VOICES FROM THE FIELD

"This book makes a compelling case for disrupting the long-standing inertia in women's health. By spotlighting creative, practical solutions, it shows how targeted pressure—and even small, smart actions—can catalyze **meaningful, scalable change in outcomes.**"

– Kalahn Taylor-Clark, PhD, MPH, vice president of Social Impact & Sustainability at Merck

"Marissa Fayer brings rare clarity to the question of women's health, positioning it as foundational infrastructure for functioning societies. The book advances a rigorous economic argument with direct relevance for leaders across healthcare, industry, and policy. **It deserves the attention** of those shaping capital allocation and system design."

– Mathias Goyen, Prof. Dr. med., chief medical officer at GE HealthCare

"*Undervalued to Unavoidable* puts into sharp focus a critical shift—from treating women's health as a cause to recognizing it as core infrastructure for functioning health systems, economies, and the lives that depend on them. ... **This is the playbook leaders need** to build resilient, high-performing systems that actually work for people."

– Komal Bajaj, MD, chief physician executive and OB-GYN Geneticist

"This isn't a book about women. It's about the largest blind spot in modern healthcare and what it's costing every economy that keeps tolerating it. *Undervalued to Unavoidable* is **the clearest argument I've read** for why the rest of us should stop treating that mystery as someone else's problem."

– Naveen Jain, founder of Viome and Moon Express

"This book gives language to what many of us have seen for years: the gaps in women's health are not isolated failures, but design problems. Drawing on her engineering background, Marissa approaches these challenges with insight, pragmatism, and a builder's mindset. She makes a compelling case that progress will require more than awareness—it will require better evidence, smarter capital, aligned incentives, and leaders willing to work across clinical, commercial, and policy silos. **This is a practical, engaging, and timely call** to build the infrastructure women's health has long needed."

– *Mitzi Krockover, MD, CEO of Woman Centered and co-founder of FemTech AZ*

"For anyone who shapes budgets, builds products, designs research, or sets policy, Undervalued to Unavoidable is essential reading. Marissa Fayer delivers what the field has long needed: **a clear, evidence-grounded framework** for embedding women's health equitably into system design from the ground up—not as an afterthought, not as a niche, but as the load-bearing infrastructure it has always been."

– *Pierre Theordore, MD, executive director at Genentech*

"For anyone who has ever sensed that something is fundamentally broken here, this book will give you **the words, the tools, and the conviction to act.**"

– *Reenita Das, healthcare changemaker and Top 100 Women in HealthTech & FemTech*

"**This is a must-read for anyone in healthcare.** As a big pharma CDO, I saw firsthand what a difference infrastructure makes to guide action. This book nailed it."

– *Jessica Federer, managing director of the Women's Health Fund*

"Marissa Fayer's **framing of women's health needs as infrastructure is both necessary and timely**. Her stories will make you infuriated at the glaring gaps in research and investment funding for women's health... This is a book that needs to be read and acted upon."

– *Esther Pan Sloane, managing director of Eyre Street Capital*

Undervalued to Unavoidable

Women's Health as Infrastructure

BY MARISSA FAYER

Undervalued to Unavoidable: Women's Health as Infrastructure

Published by Clearspan Press, an imprint of Fayer Consulting LLC
New Rochelle, New York

First Edition, 2026

ISBN 979-8-9954044-1-5 (hardcover)
ISBN 979-8-9954044-2-2 (paperback)
ISBN 979-8-9954044-0-8 (e-book)

Cover and interior design by Alma Hortelano
Editorial direction by Cecilia Meis and Katelin Walling
Produced in partnership with Lúcida, wearelucida.co

The information in this book is provided for general business and educational purposes. It is not intended as medical advice, diagnosis, or treatment, and it should not replace consultation with qualified healthcare professionals. Likewise, nothing in this book constitutes investment, legal, or financial advice. Readers should consult appropriate professionals before making decisions based on the material presented.

Bulk purchase discounts are available for corporations, associations, and educational institutions. For details, visit unavoidable.marissafayer.com/bulk.

Distributed globally through Amazon KDP and IngramSpark. Manufactured by print-on-demand in the country of distribution.

10 9 8 7 6 5 4 3 2 1

To my parents, Ella and Russ, who never put me in a box. You encouraged me to be anything I wanted, no matter how unconventional it seemed at the time. Because of your openness and bravery, hundreds of thousands (if not millions) of women around the world have better health today and into the future.

CONTENTS

PROLOGUE: THE OX IN THE ROAD

It started in a bar in Costa Rica in 2010.

I was living there at the time, working for Hologic, the largest mammography equipment manufacturer in the world. It was a normal night, and I was having a drink with my friend, Victoria Ross, who ran Fundación Dra. Anna Ross, which was the largest breast cancer charity in the country. She told me about women dying of breast cancer in the eastern region of the country because the only mammography machine in the entire region had been broken for years. Women had stopped getting screened for a disease that, when caught early, has a five-year survival rate of 99 percent They were dying because a machine broke and nobody came to fix it.

I knew, because it was literally my job to know, that there was working equipment sitting in warehouses in the United States. Machines that had been replaced by newer models but still functioned perfectly. Equipment I had personally rolled into dumpsters to make room for new inventory. Functional machines going into landfills while women hours away from where I was sitting were dying without them.

So I said what felt obvious at the time: "Let's get you one."

I had no idea how to *actually* do it. I didn't know how to get a mammography machine out of a US warehouse, into Costa Rica, and over treacherous mountain roads, let alone install it without sufficient power lines in place and get people trained and doctors to use it. But I took the leap and made the commitment to solve the problem.

It took dozens of meetings with the Costa Rican government and several more meetings with the US Embassy to help get it into the country as diplomatic cargo. At the same time, I was about to leave

Costa Rica and move to Canada for another assignment within the same company. Time was ticking. When the machine arrived in the airport, we had to fill out more paperwork and explain the situation a dozen more times. After four months, the equipment was released from the Costa Rican warehouse

We did it. Working together with the manufacturer, the local Costa Rican facility, the government and health ministry of Costa Rica, the US Embassy, Fundación Dra. Anna Gabriela Ross, and the regional hospital, we installed a repurposed mammography machine where women hadn't been screened in years. After five years of use, the mortality rate in that region dropped to approximately ten times lower than it had been. What was outdated inventory in one country was life-saving infrastructure in another.

Now multiply that outcome across every region where the same gap exists. That's the scale of what we're leaving on the table.

Women's health is the infrastructure that holds healthy, functioning societies together. Treating it as a specialty, a niche, a side conversation, or a moment in time has cost the global economies trillions and counting.

> What was outdated inventory in one country was life-saving infrastructure in another.

Women make up half the world's population, the majority of the global healthcare workforce, and the bulk of unpaid caregivers. When women are healthy, systems work. When they're not, everything downstream fractures: productivity, education, household stability, labor markets, gross domestic product (GDP).

McKinsey Health Institute estimates that closing the women's health gap represents a trillion-dollar opportunity annually. That figure is a floor, not a ceiling.

And yet, women's health has only ever been treated like an exception—something to address after other priorities are funded. It's been intentionally split into specialties, scattered across disciplines, and framed in ways that make it difficult to see the whole system.

You may be running a company and sensing that something in how women's health is approached doesn't add up, but you can't quite name it. You may be a policymaker who keeps hearing about women's health as a moral issue and have never once seen it framed as what it actually is: an infrastructure problem with a massive economic consequence. You might care deeply and still feel unsure where you fit.

That confusion isn't a personal failure. It's a feature of how the system has been designed.

I was you.

I didn't know where to start. I didn't know how interconnected everything was. I didn't know how much opportunity existed—not just to fix what was broken, but to redesign systems entirely. But I did know that my gut was telling me something felt fundamentally wrong: half of the population didn't have what it needed to thrive. I was working inside an industry that was helping people have better health. But until that conversation in the Costa Rican bar, I didn't realize how many people were being left behind if they weren't able to spend copious amounts of money on the newest innovations and equipment. Waiting for someone else to address it wasn't working.

That realization crystallized one morning on my drive to the office in Costa Rica, when the road came to a complete stop. Standing directly in my path was an enormous ox—motionless, heavy, and entirely unconcerned with the fact that it was blocking the only way forward.

I waited and waited but nothing happened. I eventually called my closest friend Kenneth, who lived in Costa Rica his entire life. He just laughed and told me to inch forward and honk: "It needs to see you. And don't be quiet. Be loud."

Slowly, deliberately, I edged the car forward and leaned on the horn. The ox lifted its head, acknowledged my presence, and stepped aside just enough for me to pass.

At the time, it felt like an anecdote, which I laugh about to this day. In hindsight, it was a blueprint. That ox represents the system: heavy, entrenched, normalized, and built for a different time. It wasn't malicious. It was inert, and it wasn't going to move unless someone applied pressure.

That is women's health.

Global health systems are filled with oxen. Structures designed around male biology, male life trajectories, and male assumptions. Research agendas that treat women as deviations from a default. Funding priorities that underinvest in conditions affecting women. Policies that rely on women's unpaid labor while failing to protect their health.

These systems don't change themselves. They move when pressure is applied.

For decades, women have absorbed the cost of this inertia—with their bodies, their careers, and their health—while societies functioned just well enough to avoid collapse. That invisible subsidy has kept systems running while eroding their foundation.

Despite the magnitude of the problem, the path forward is clearer than most people realize. Women's health is one of the highest return investments available today across multiple fronts: economic, social, demographic, and generational. Countries that invest in women's health grow faster. Companies that integrate women into leadership perform better. Health systems that address women's needs become more efficient, more sustainable, and more equitable overall.

You may not think of yourself as someone who shapes women's health or who can make any difference at all. Most people don't. But if you influence budgets, products, policies, research agendas, workplaces, or institutions, you already do whether you intend to or not.

The ox is moving, but not fast enough.

It's time to see women's health clearly—not as a cause, but as the load-bearing infrastructure of thriving societies.

Once you do, there is no going back.

PART I: THE LANDSCAPE

Let me start by painting a picture of the state of women's health. There's a lot to take in and understand. There will be a lot of facts and information in the next few chapters. It's overwhelming, but it enables you to level-set, understand the problem, and recognize there are solutions, which we will get to. This information helps create the grounding for use of this information when and however you need it. I promise that everything isn't doom and gloom... well maybe this section is, but the rest of the book is filled with solutions and changes you can make.

I've sat in boardrooms where these statistics were presented as abstractions to the people with the power to change them, and I've sat in clinics where they were someone's lived truth. This illustrates the reality of women's health, the lack and the opportunity. I've seen all sides of the industry and know there are better ways of operating to ensure women have access to better health.

Chapter 1: **Global Snapshot**

More than 10 years ago, I took my first trip to Arusha, Tanzania to discuss a new project with clinic administrators. At this point, I had been living in Latin America for many years, so I understood the scope of what developing country healthcare clinics look like. That isn't the story. On my first day in the city, a local healthcare partner brought me to the women's health area of the clinic I was visiting.

Forty pregnant women were waiting on benches outside the clinic at 9 o'clock in the morning. Many had bedrolls next to them and at least one child on their hip. I naively asked how everyone arrived so early. The head nurse of the local facility, who walked me around the clinic, explained that most of the women had been there since yesterday. Five of them were there from the day before. Clearly I looked surprised; she explained that due to the lack of maternal health screening clinics in the more remote regions of the city, they walked, rode buses, or took boda-bodas (motorbikes that are used like taxis) to be seen once at the clinic throughout their pregnancies.

It was a luxury for them to even come to the clinic that one time, as they were the "lucky" women with the means to be seen and the education to know they needed to do so. They live the reality of seeing friends, family members, and often themselves having difficult births.

The next closest clinic was more than 20 miles away (32 kilometers). This building had running water and electricity. Supplies were low but available. Several of the nurses on duty were exhausted and had already been working for eighteen hours straight in the labor and delivery ward. For each of these women, having a child shouldn't be a medical event. But the reality is, it's a gamble with their lives. Their chance of dying in labor is about one in thirty-seven. If any of them lived in a high-income country (HIC) such as Norway or Australia, her odds would be closer to one in 4,900.

This experience is an everyday reality for millions of women around the world. It's the story of systemic design failure: healthcare built for half the population (men) but not designed with the other half of the population (women) in mind.

Women make up half of humanity but remain the most underserved group in global health systems. The reasons lie in the politics, economics, and priorities that shape care delivery.

This book is focused on all aspects of women's health and healthcare, not just maternal health. This includes longevity, well-being, healthy living, and creating societies that incorporate women and their health in all aspects of life. But most importantly, this has to do with the economic opportunity we have to improve women's health globally.

Women make up half of humanity but remain the most underserved group in global health systems.

The Longer Life Paradox

Women's longevity is one of the world's great medical achievements—and one of its cruelest ironies. Women now live an average of five years longer than men but spend those extra years in poorer health. According to the Global Burden of Disease study, women experience more years of disability and chronic illness across nearly every region.

Why? Because health systems still define women's health primarily through reproduction. Once a woman passes childbearing age, she all but disappears from the data. Yet the majority of health problems she'll face—heart disease, cancer, diabetes, osteoporosis, depression—emerge after her reproductive years.

Cardiovascular disease kills more women each year than all cancers combined. Globally, it's the leading killer of women. Yet because symptoms in women often differ from those in men, heart disease is underdiagnosed, undertreated, and underestimated in women. In many clinical settings, a woman experiencing chest discomfort or fatigue is told she's "anxious" and sent home.

Cancer tells a similar story. Approximately 2.3 million women around the world are diagnosed with breast cancer annually, and cervical cancer still claims roughly 348,000 lives each year globally. The tragedy is, most cervical cancers are preventable with vaccination and screening. But access is uneven. Australia, which has universal HPV vaccination and regular screenings, is on track to eliminate cervical cancer within a decade. Meanwhile, women in low-income countries (LICs), where 90 percent of deaths occur, face barriers that are as much political as medical: weak healthcare systems, vaccine costs, and cultural stigma.

These conditions are not "women's problems." They're global health problems. But without data disaggregated by sex, inclusion in clinical trials, and research funding that reflects women's disease burden, they remain invisible.

Health Systems Built Without Women in Mind

Across nearly every measure of access, equity, and outcomes, women fare worse than men. The World Health Organization and World Bank estimate that half of the world's people still lack access to essential health services. Within that half, women are disproportionately affected by cost, geography, cultural barriers, and discrimination.

Every year, 287,000 women globally die from maternal causes, yet nearly all of these deaths are preventable. Around 70 percent occur in sub-Saharan Africa, where weak infrastructure, shortages of trained professionals, and supply-chain disruptions make safe delivery a privilege rather than a right. These are deaths from hemorrhage, infection, untreated hypertension, and lack of timely care, not rare complications.

Meanwhile, 270 million women globally have an unmet need for modern contraception. That means nearly one in ten women of reproductive age wants to avoid pregnancy but can't access safe, affordable, or acceptable options. Behind those numbers are real consequences: unintended pregnancies, unsafe abortions, and lost opportunities for education and work.

Cardiovascular disease reveals how systems are mis-designed. Women experience different symptoms than men, yet care protocols still reflect male patterns. Each year, more than 9 million women around the world die from cardiovascular disease, and many more are misdiagnosed or treated too late, leading to worse outcomes than men.

Intersecting Barriers: Geography, Poverty, and Gender

Inequity is rarely driven by one factor. Geography, income, education, and gender amplify one another in complex ways.

In sub-Saharan Africa and South Asia, maternal mortality rates remain high, not just because of medical gaps, but because of broader social inequities. Girls who marry before eighteen are more likely to die in childbirth. Women who lack education are less likely to access antenatal care. Minor complications can become fatal where transport is unreliable or non-existent.

> Across all regions, the underlying pattern is consistent: women's health outcomes improve where equity is prioritized as a policy goal, not treated as a secondary benefit.

In parts of the Middle East and North Africa, mobility restrictions limit women's ability to seek care. Across low- and middle-income countries (LMICs), out-of-pocket payments for healthcare can consume a family's entire income. When money is short, women and girls are often the ones who go without.

Even in HICs, inequities persist. In the US, Black women are three times more likely to die from pregnancy-related causes than white women, even after adjusting for income and education. Indigenous women in Canada and Australia experience similar disparities. These are not gaps of knowledge. They are gaps of value and design.

Across all regions, the underlying pattern is consistent: women's health outcomes improve where equity is prioritized as a policy goal, not treated as a secondary benefit.

The Hidden Cost of Neglect

When women's health is ignored, the losses cascade far beyond the clinic. The economic costs are staggering. The World Bank estimates that gender inequality in health and work costs the global economy trillions of dollars each year. Advancing gender equality represents one of the largest untapped economic opportunities in the world. The McKinsey Global Institute estimates that closing gender gaps could add roughly $12 trillion to the global economy and as much as $28 trillion with full gender parity.

The opportunity cost is just as striking. There's a nine-time return on investment in women's and children's health. A dollar invested in family planning saves $2-$6 in healthcare costs down the line. Investments in nutrition yield returns of sixteen to one in productivity and income.

In purely financial terms, the return on investment in women's health outperforms nearly every other development strategy.

The business case is unambiguous. Ignoring women's health isn't only unjust. It's economically irrational. Yet too often, decision-makers still view women's health through the lens of morality or charity, not economics.

> Ignoring women's health isn't only unjust. It's economically irrational.

Changing the Data: Who Gets Counted, Who Gets Cared For

Progress requires information, and data remains one of the most persistent barriers to women's health equity. Even today, global health datasets often fail to disaggregate outcomes by sex, gender, or socioeconomic status. Without that detail, policymakers and investors can't see where the gaps truly are.

In research, the bias runs deep. Women were excluded from most clinical trials until 1993.

This lack of data is lethal. It means that diagnostic criteria, treatment guidelines, and medical devices are all optimized for male physiology. The result? Women's symptoms are misdiagnosed or dismissed, and their outcomes suffer.

The fix is straightforward: mandate gender-disaggregated data, require balanced participation in trials, and fund research that examines sex-based differences in disease.

Because when women are counted, they are cared for.

Signals of a Flawed System

What emerges from this global snapshot is not simply a collection of health disparities. Across continents, income levels, and political systems, the same gaps appear again and again: women living longer but sicker, diseases overlooked because symptoms differ from men's, research pipelines excluding half the population, and health systems prioritizing reproduction but neglecting the decades that follow.

These aren't isolated failures. They're signals of a system that was never fully designed with women in mind.

And design failures are important for one reason: they can be fixed.

Once we stop treating women's health gaps as unfortunate outcomes and start recognizing them as structural choices, the conversation changes. The issue is no longer whether the world cares enough about women's health. The issue is how the institutions that shape health—research, policy, funding, and leadership—were built in the first place.

Chapter 1 Takeaways

- **WOMEN'S HEALTH GAPS ARE SYSTEMIC DESIGN FAILURES.** MODERN HEALTH SYSTEMS WERE BUILT AROUND MALE DATA, MALE BODIES, AND MALE PRIORITIES.
- **WOMEN LIVE LONGER THAN MEN BUT SPEND MORE YEARS IN POOR HEALTH.** THE DECADES OF DISEASE RISK AFTER REPRODUCTION REMAIN UNDER-RESEARCHED, UNDERDIAGNOSED, AND UNDERFUNDED.
- **IGNORING WOMEN'S HEALTH IS ECONOMICALLY IRRATIONAL.** INVESTMENTS IN WOMEN'S HEALTH DELIVER SOME OF THE HIGHEST RETURNS IN GLOBAL DEVELOPMENT AND ECONOMIC GROWTH.
- **WHO GETS COUNTED DETERMINES WHO GETS CARE.** WHEN WOMEN ARE MISSING FROM RESEARCH, DATA, AND LEADERSHIP, THEIR HEALTH NEEDS REMAIN INVISIBLE, AND SYSTEMS CONTINUE TO FAIL HALF THE POPULATION.

Chapter 2: **It's Structural**

In 1991, Dr. Bernadine Healy became the first woman to lead the National Institutes of Health. Her first major public statement, an editorial in *the New England Journal of Medicine*, named what researchers had quietly documented for years: women had been excluded from most major clinical trials on heart disease, even though heart disease was, and still is, the leading cause of death among American women. The omission wasn't accidental.

For decades, researchers assumed that what worked in men would work in women. Male anatomy became the model in textbooks. Male physiology set the dosing standards for drugs. Male-centric symptoms defined what "disease" looked like. When female anatomy, physiology, and symptoms didn't fit the pattern, the system didn't adapt. Women were simply told they were "atypical."

The fallout was predictable and deadly. Women's heart attacks went undiagnosed because they presented differently. Drugs metabolized differently in women, sometimes with severe side effects. Pain was dismissed as anxiety or "hormonal." Because of these findings, women were finally included in clinical studies in 1993.

The problem wasn't individual prejudice. It was design.

Modern medicine was built around male biology, and women were expected to fit that model to receive appropriate care. As Healy explained, women are more likely to be treated less aggressively than men until they prove that they're as sick as men.

Her words still resonate. Systems reflect their architects, and for most of modern medical history, those architects were men.

The Invisible Default

Women's exclusion from research wasn't just a historical oversight. It became the invisible foundation of modern healthcare. The data we rely on, the protocols we follow, and even the technologies we celebrate all carry that bias forward.

Today, only 9 to 11 percent of US medical research funding targets conditions specific to women, despite women representing half the population and carrying a substantial share of disease burden. And that's higher than the few countries that track this data, including Canada, the UK, and the European Union.

That funding imbalance widens the research gaps. Women remain underrepresented in clinical trials, making up fewer than 40 percent of participants in cardiovascular research and less than 30 percent in many cancer and mental health studies. The result is predictable: diseases that primarily affect women remain poorly understood, underdiagnosed, and undertreated. Endometriosis, for example, affects more than 190 million women worldwide, yet diagnostic tools remain crude and treatment options are limited.

> Today, only 9–11% of US medical research funding targets conditions specific to women.

But bias doesn't always announce itself. Sometimes it lives quietly inside the architecture of how systems work, from funding formulas to procurement processes to who sits at the table when decisions are made:

- Grant mechanisms often favor large, established research centers, which are overwhelmingly led by men.
- Medical school curricula still allocate far more hours to male-centric anatomy than to female-specific health.
- Procurement systems for hospitals reward bulk purchasing over community relevance, sidelining women-led innovations that don't yet scale.
- Policy frameworks routinely ignore gender impacts—as seen most recently during the pandemic, when fewer than half of national COVID-19 responses integrated gender considerations.

Many of these structural features may seem neutral, but their outcomes are not. The consequences of these inequities are visible in every metric that matters. Women are misdiagnosed more often, treated later, and excluded from trials that inform care standards. For example, women with the same levels of pain as men are less likely to receive opioid analgesics in emergency departments, resulting in undertreatment of acute pain.

In global health systems, the inequity is even sharper. In many LMICs, the gender imbalance in funding, training, and data collection leaves women under-cared-for and overburdened. They deliver the majority of unpaid and underpaid care while lacking access to healthcare themselves.

In Pakistan, menopause has largely gone unmeasured. National surveys don't ask the right questions, clinical systems don't code symptoms in a consistent way, and cultural norms often keep the conversation out of formal health settings. That's the gap Zainab Wadood set out to address in the spring of 2026 with the launch of Insights Engine, which collects data directly from Pakistani women to make this life stage visible for the first time.

That absence of data has real consequences. If symptoms aren't tracked and counted, they don't show up in clinical guidelines, reimbursement models, or product development pipelines. What looks like a lack of demand is actually a lack of visibility.

Working to resolve these inequities, redesign the system, and scale for women's health is a challenge throughout innovators and operators' careers.

The structure of access itself can be discriminatory.

A System Built on Power, Not Performance

Bias in healthcare is the predictable outcome of power. Those who set research priorities, approve budgets, and design policies shape what gets studied, funded, and delivered. When women are excluded from leadership, women's health remains an afterthought.

Women make up 70 percent of the global health workforce, yet only one in four holds a leadership role. They run the wards but not the budgets. They are the hands and hearts of the system but rarely its architects.

In one regional hospital in Nairobi I visited in 2017, a nurse who had been practicing for more than 20 years told me she'd trained six of the men who are now running her department. She knows every detail of that emergency department and hospital. "They went off for leadership courses, and I covered their shifts," she said. She never received the same opportunity.

This pattern is global. The hierarchies of healthcare—from hospitals to health ministries—mirror the power structures of the societies they serve. Women's work is valued as service, not strategy. Their leadership is framed as exception, not expectation.

> Women are more likely to experience adverse drug reactions, sometimes at twice the rate of men.

The Three Challenges Destroying Women's Healthcare

In *A New Vision for Women's Health Research: Transformative Change at the National Institutes of Health*, the National Academies of Sciences, Engineering, and Medicine outlined three interlocking crises that continue to erode women's health globally.

1. KNOWLEDGE GAPS IN RESEARCH

Despite decades of advocacy, most research pipelines still exclude or underrepresent women. Sex-based differences in immunity, metabolism, and disease progression remain poorly understood. Pharmaceutical trials still rely on male-dominated cohorts, and the lack of disaggregated data means even well-intentioned policies are built on incomplete evidence.

The consequences are tangible. Women are more likely to experience adverse drug reactions, sometimes at twice the rate of men.

The sleeping pill Ambien became infamous for causing severe morning drowsiness in women until dosage guidelines were halved after years of reports.

The same issue exists across cardiovascular, psychiatric, and pain medications. In many cases, women are overmedicated, underdiagnosed, or mis-prescribed.

A 2024 article in *Current Research in Pharmacology and Drug Discovery* called for an overhaul of pharmacological research, noting that sex should be considered from the preclinical stage onward.

2. WORKFORCE IN CRISIS

Healthcare runs on women's labor, from nurses and midwives to community health workers. Yet this workforce is stretched to a breaking point. Women are concentrated in the lowest-paid roles, face higher rates of workplace violence, and are often excluded from policy tables that determine working conditions. Burnout, moral injury, and migration out of the sector threaten the stability of global healthcare systems.

During the pandemic, hospitals depended almost entirely on nurses, midwives, and community health workers—roles overwhelmingly filled by women. They sacrificed being with their families and lived in their garages, hotels, and even short-term rentals to protect their families during the beginning of the crisis. Yet when staffing rules, budgets, and safety policies were debated, the voices in the room were far more likely to be administrators than the women delivering care.

When a system's most essential workers are undervalued, quality declines across the board. The workforce crisis is gender-driven, not gender-neutral.

3. AN INNOVATION DEFICIT

Innovation in women's health lags far behind other fields. Medical devices and drugs are still designed primarily for male bodies. Global venture funding for women's health startups remains below 2 percent of total health investment. Even the language of innovation often sidelines women as "niche markets," "low-growth categories," or "non-critical segments."

After listening to a female scientist at a biotech firm speak at a conference several years ago, Sophia Franklin (her name has been changed to protect her identity) told me she had to "fight for permission" to include menstrual-cycle tracking in her cardiovascular study because it was deemed a "confounding variable."

"The confounder," she said, "is pretending we're all the same."

These crises share a common root: power asymmetry. When men dominate leadership, women's health is consistently underfunded, undervalued, and misunderstood. Power determines what is visible, measurable, and worthy of investment.

> When men dominate leadership, women's health is consistently underfunded, undervalued, and misunderstood.

AI: The New Mirror of Bias

Artificial intelligence (AI) is being hailed as the future of healthcare, but it's only as fair as the data it learns from. When that data excludes women, so will the algorithms that depend on it.

In one study published in *PNAS*, medical imaging algorithms trained on male-dominant datasets performed significantly worse when diagnosing female patients. The technology wasn't intentionally biased. It simply learned from data that reflected decades of male-centered medical research.

When algorithms are blind to gender, they don't just replicate bias, they automate it. This is also true when it's blind to ethnicity, geography, and socioeconomic factors. In the companies I work with and advise, I've made it a priority that women of all ethnicities from multiple geographic regions are included in studies and trials, and I've stated publicly that I will not authorize a study without diversity in the training data. At DeepLook Medical, the breast cancer imaging company I'm CEO of, we write into clinical study protocols that participants must be diverse, outlining the percentage breakdown by ethnicity.

Because a solution that hasn't been tested on the people it's built for is just another version of the status quo. AI trained with biased data will continue to perpetuate the bias that is already pervasive in the system.

Yet the potential for good is enormous. AI could close diagnostic gaps that have persisted for generations. What matters is who designs it and whose data trains it.

When women scientists, engineers, and clinicians are at the table, outcomes shift. Technology itself isn't the problem; the absence of representation is.

AI has the power to rewrite medicine's story if we don't let it copy the old one.

Compounding Consequences

The inequities in women's health are structural. The system was built on the default where research, funding, leadership, and innovation pipelines were structured around men's bodies and experiences, with women added later—if at all. When those structural choices compound over decades, the result is predictable: women are studied less, diagnosed later, treated differently, and often misunderstood by the very systems meant to care for them.

And structural exclusion has consequences far beyond policy or funding decisions. It shapes the diseases that are recognized, the symptoms that are believed, the drugs that are tested, and the care women receive throughout their lives. To understand the true cost of this design, we must look at what those systems have produced in women's actual health outcomes.

Chapter 2 Takeaways

- **MODERN MEDICINE WAS BUILT ON A MALE DEFAULT.** RESEARCH, DIAGNOSTICS, AND TREATMENT PROTOCOLS WERE DESIGNED AROUND MALE BIOLOGY, LEAVING WOMEN MISDIAGNOSED, UNDERTREATED, AND MISUNDERSTOOD.
- **BIAS IN HEALTHCARE IS STRUCTURAL, NOT ACCIDENTAL.** FUNDING PRIORITIES, CLINICAL TRIALS, PROCUREMENT SYSTEMS, AND POLICY FRAMEWORKS SYSTEMATICALLY UNDERINVEST IN WOMEN'S HEALTH.
- **WOMEN POWER THE HEALTHCARE WORKFORCE BUT RARELY CONTROL THE SYSTEM.** THEY MAKE UP ABOUT 70 PERCENT OF THE GLOBAL HEALTH WORKFORCE YET HOLD ONLY A FRACTION OF LEADERSHIP ROLES THAT DETERMINE FUNDING, RESEARCH, AND POLICY.
- **TECHNOLOGY WILL EITHER CORRECT BIAS OR SCALE IT.** AI AND NEW HEALTH TECHNOLOGIES WILL REPRODUCE THE SAME INEQUITIES UNLESS WOMEN ARE INCLUDED IN THE DATA, DESIGN, AND LEADERSHIP SHAPING THEM.

Chapter 3: **The Scope Beyond Fertility**

During a routine annual mammogram in early 2025 at a New York City hospital, one that's considered among the best in the world, the radiologist saw something they didn't like or couldn't visualize in my imaging. Now I know it was because, like 50 percent of women globally, I have dense breast tissue. I've worked in breast imaging for more than a decade and currently lead a company that specializes in dense breast tissue imaging. So logically, I'll routinely need extra imaging, likely have many "scares," and will need to be extra vigilant. But when I heard those words, I stopped in my tracks. I was terrified of the unknown.

Because of the backlog, my appointment for a diagnostic ultrasound and second mammogram was scheduled for three weeks later. I "knew" I was fine, but my nervous system didn't. For three weeks, I was semi-non-productive, racked with worry, and overanalyzed everything.

Due to the location of the area getting re-checked, I needed a spot mammogram, which applies increased pressure to a specific area for better visualization—the same technology I helped create more than fifteen years ago. I know the process. I know the machines. I know how it all works. But I was *still* scared.

I walked out of the appointment with a massive bruise on my left breast that lasted for weeks, and I was unable to move that side of my body without intense pain for days. Thankfully, that spot was exactly what I intellectually knew was the truth: I have dense breasts, and the radiologist couldn't clearly see a certain area and needed to "double check."

I knew what was happening and why, but it made me think about the women across the globe who don't know this space as well as I do. How must they feel? Do they ever go back for additional imaging? Will they go back next year knowing this could happen again?

When people hear the phrase "women's health," most think of reproduction. It's instinctive—the imagery of pregnancy, fertility treatments, and childbirth. Health campaigns show smiling expectant mothers or newborns wrapped in pink. Policy papers lump "maternal and child health" into a single line item, as if women's health begins and ends with motherhood.

But the greatest health risks (like my dense breast tissue) for most women on this planet come long after or far beyond fertility. The leading causes of death for women globally aren't childbirth or infectious disease. The data dismantles that myth. Women are much more likely to die from heart disease, cancer, stroke, and other chronic conditions. These are the same diseases that dominate health systems for men yet are misdiagnosed in women because they often manifest differently and remain drastically underfunded.

Cardiovascular disease (CVD) is the number one killer of women worldwide, accounting for roughly 35 percent of female deaths. That's more than all cancers combined, though cancer follows closely. Breast cancer is the most common cancer among women, with 677,000 deaths globally.

The greatest health risks for most women on this planet come long after or far beyond fertility.

Other non-communicable diseases (NCDs) like autoimmune disorders, osteoporosis, diabetes, and mental health conditions create massive, lifelong burdens. Women represent 80 percent of autoimmune disease cases, are twice as likely to experience major depression or anxiety, and half of women older than fifty will break a bone from osteoporosis.

The rise of NCDs is the most significant—and least discussed—shift in global health in the last fifty years. Once dominated by infectious disease and maternal mortality, women's health now faces a global chronic disease crisis that outpaces the system's imagination.

According to the World Health Organization, three out of every four female deaths worldwide are now due to NCDs. The pattern is clear:

- In high-income countries, chronic disease shortens women's healthy years.
- In middle-income countries, lifestyle risk factors (diet, inactivity, and tobacco use) combined with limited access to early detection are the culprit.
- In low-income countries, women often experience a double burden: persistent maternal mortality on top of rising chronic illness, with few systems capable of handling both.

Yet when funding proposals talk about "women's health," NCDs are rarely mentioned. Most national women's health strategies still devote the majority of their funding and focus on reproductive services.

In March 2026, I spoke at a women's global health meeting during the UN Commission on the Status of Women alongside a global health leader who leads several Nordic countries at one the largest pharmaceutical companies in the world. She put it bluntly: "We have entire ministries of health built around fertility and none built around female aging. That needs to change."

The irony is brutal: women live longer than men but spend far more of those years in poor health. And still, systems treat them as if the only part of their bodies that matter is the one that gives life.

Heart Disease: The Invisible Killer

Cardiovascular disease has long been considered a "man's problem." The imagery—the businessman clutching his chest, the smoker with high cholesterol—was shaped around men's experiences. Today, cardiovascular disease remains the leading cause of death among women globally, responsible for nearly 9 million deaths each year.

The symptoms differ. Women's heart attacks are often quieter—shortness of breath, fatigue, back or jaw pain, nausea—yet deadly when overlooked. Women are more likely to be told it's anxiety, stress, or menopause and sent home from emergency departments.

The European Society of Cardiology found that women experiencing heart attacks were 50 percent more likely than men to receive an incorrect initial diagnosis. In the US, women wait an average of 11 minutes longer for life-saving treatment once they arrive at a hospital. That seems like a short duration of time, but every second counts during a heart attack.

Hormonal transitions, like pregnancy complications or changes due to menopause, add layers of risk. Women with preeclampsia are twice as likely to develop heart disease later in life. Yet obstetricians rarely flag this long-term link, and cardiologists rarely ask about reproductive history. Sadly, there isn't enough data about heart disease related to menopausal hormone changes.

But the messaging is failing them, not the medicine.

> The messaging about CVD is failing women, not the medicine.

Cancer: Progress and Paradox

Cancer tells another story of progress laced with inequity.

In wealthy nations, breast cancer survival rates now exceed 90 percent thanks to early detection and treatment advances. But in low- and middle-income countries, survival drops below 50 percent because women are diagnosed late—like in that remote region of Costa Rica that had the broken mammography machine—or can't afford care.

Cervical cancer, almost entirely preventable through HPV vaccination, remains a death sentence in much of the Global South. Despite global commitments to eliminate it by 2030, vaccination coverage lags far behind. Australia is on track to eradicate cervical cancer within the next decade. Meanwhile, it remains one of the top three causes of female death in Sub-Saharan Africa.

That's because it's not treated as a priority.

Pharmaceutical companies and governments pour billions into fertility treatments yet balk at the logistics of delivering a $5 HPV vaccine to adolescent girls in rural clinics.

The WHO's global cervical cancer elimination strategy estimates that every $1 invested in HPV vaccination and screening yields a $3.20 return in productivity and healthcare savings. Yet the funding gaps persist.

Cancer is the starkest reminder that innovation alone doesn't guarantee equity. Without intentional design for distribution, it widens the gap between those who can access it and those who can't.

Autoimmune Disorders: The Body at War with Itself

If heart disease and cancer represent the visible threats, autoimmune diseases are the invisible ones. These are conditions where the immune system mistakenly attacks the body's own tissues—often devastating, often misunderstood, and overwhelmingly female.

Lupus, rheumatoid arthritis, multiple sclerosis, thyroid disorders—the list is long, and so is the neglect. Women represent four in five autoimmune diagnoses, yet research funding in this category remains disproportionately low.

Because these conditions rarely kill quickly, they fall outside the traditional "burden of disease" metrics that drive funding. But they rob women of their quality of life, ability to work, and economic independence.

Autoimmune diseases often strike in early adulthood when women are balancing careers and family life. Symptoms are subtle, fluctuating, and easily dismissed: fatigue, joint pain, cognitive fog. Many women spend years seeking a diagnosis, cycling through specialists who treat each symptom in isolation.

As lupus patients often say, the hardest part isn't the disease. It's convincing people it's real.

Mental Health: The Mind-Body Divide

No condition better exposes gender bias in medicine than mental health. Depression and anxiety affect women nearly twice as often as men. Yet the causes—biological, social, and economic—are intertwined in ways most systems still fail to address.

The WHO estimates that that 6.9 percent of women will experience a major depressive episode in their lifetime. Adolescent girls and women in early adulthood face the highest risk. In LMICs, depression is now one of the top five causes of disability among women.

But diagnosis and treatment are riddled with inequity. In wealthier nations, women are overprescribed antidepressants, often as a quick fix for undiagnosed thyroid disease, menopause, or chronic pain. In poorer regions, women receive no treatment at all.

The National Institute of Mental Health notes that hormonal fluctuations—menstruation, pregnancy, postpartum, and menopause—amplify vulnerability, yet most mental health protocols ignore these differences. Women's mental health is either pathologized or trivialized. Postpartum depression becomes "baby blues." Menopause-related anxiety becomes "anger." The message to women is consistent: your suffering is emotional, not medical.

Mental health is a pillar of overall well-being, not an afterthought of reproductive health. When it fails, the consequences ripple far beyond the individual. Depression and anxiety alone cost the global economy nearly $1 trillion each year in lost productivity, underscoring how untreated mental health challenges destabilize families, workplaces, and communities.

Aging, Menopause, and the Unspoken Decades

There's a silent stretch in most women's health journeys: the decades after childbearing but before old age. Menopause marks a biological transition, but health systems treat it like an afterthought.

Hot flashes, insomnia, cognitive changes, and other physical changes affect hundreds of millions of women. Yet most receive little guidance, and only a small percentage are offered hormone therapy or alternative management.

A 2022 Fawcett Society study found that 77 percent of British women experience one or more menopausal symptoms affecting work and quality of life, yet 42 percent of women aged fifty-two to fifty-five hadn't discussed menopause with their provider. Even fewer receive appropriate treatment.

Yet the economic consequences are increasingly measurable. In the UK alone, menopause-related absenteeism is estimated to cost the economy £1.8 billion each year. And the scale of the issue is global. By

2030, roughly 1.2 billion women worldwide will be postmenopausal, with 47 million entering menopause each year. As women remain in the workforce longer across high-, middle-, and low-income countries, unmanaged symptoms—from sleep disruption to cognitive fog—are beginning to take a toll on labor markets. Surveys suggest one in ten women have left a job because of menopause symptoms, highlighting the growing economic cost of treating midlife health as an afterthought.

Meanwhile, osteoporosis is one of the most predictable and preventable epidemics of aging women. Yet it remains sidelined as a "normal" consequence of getting older.

Half of all women older than 50 will break a bone due to osteoporosis. A quarter of those fractures will lead to long-term disability, and one in five hip-fracture patients die within a year.

> Ignoring women age 50 and older is economically absurd.

In many cultures, frailty in older women is seen as an inevitability, not a public health failure. But bone health isn't destiny; it's policy. Regular bone-density testing, adequate calcium and vitamin D intake, and hormone management could prevent millions of fractures each year. And yet, bone health rarely appears in women's health policy.

The demographic shift is undeniable. Women older than 50 make up nearly a quarter of the world's female population. By 2030, women are projected to account for more than half of the world's people aged 50 and older. Ignoring them is economically absurd.

A Culture of Dismissal

Four years ago, I started to have horrible headaches and migraines pretty regularly—something I'd never experienced before. As the CEO of two companies, I was working and traveling constantly. My primary care doctors and several neurologists wrote it off as stress and told me I should spend more time relaxing, meditating, and sleeping. But in my gut, I knew that wasn't the issue. Something wasn't right, but I didn't know what.

I continuously advocated for myself, seeing six doctors, one dentist, and many experts for consultations, getting dozens of tests and three MRI scans of my brain. I finally saw a specialty headache physician with the neurology clinic at the largest hospital in New York City who diagnosed me with chronic migraine and daily persistent headache. The likely cause? Eight months prior, I told my primary care physician I was in perimenopause. She wanted to run some tests to confirm, which meant I had to stop taking the hormone birth control I was on for twenty-five years. That drastic hormonal shift triggered the headaches and migraines, and there's no way to "turn them back off."

After more than a year of trial-and-error, we thankfully found a treatment plan that works and I'm in the management mode of symptoms and pain. But because some of my doctors weren't trained in women's health, they didn't know the side effects women in their forties experience when they stop medications that manage hormones. Those doctors continuously told me to change jobs, take a break, get more sleep, and stop traveling so much. I knew those weren't the right solutions and I was being dismissed.

Across continents, women tell remarkably similar stories:

"I was told it was anxiety." But it was post-partum depression.

"I was told I was too young." But it was breast cancer in her thirties.

"I was told to lose weight." But it was an autoimmune disease.

From rural Kenya to New York City, from factory workers to executives, the pattern repeats: symptoms are minimized and pain is normalized.

An article in *the Lancet Rheumatology* called this "medical gaslighting"—when a woman's complaints are dismissed or attributed to mental or emotional causes rather than biological ones. This gap delays treatment and costs lives.

Expanding the Frame

Beneath all the numbers lies something deeper: infrastructure.

Women are the backbone of health systems as nurses, caregivers, and community leaders, yet their own health is secondary. They keep the world alive while their own care is rationed.

From adolescence through menopause and aging, women's health needs shift dramatically. But systems rarely follow that continuum. Many societies still tie a woman's value to her reproductive function. There's a surge of attention during reproductive years, then near silence. Policies, philanthropy, and even religious charities are comfortable funding prenatal care, but not menopause support. Few programs target post-menopausal health in LMICs, though this demographic is growing rapidly and increasingly at risk for chronic disease.

Recognizing that imbalance is a correction.

To move forward, we must dismantle the binary of "maternal versus other." If we continue defining women's health through reproduction, we will keep losing women in the prime of their lives to heart disease, cancer, mental illness, and bone fractures that could have been prevented.

But if we expand the frame, everything changes. If the same urgency and funding that go into family planning were applied to preventing heart attacks, screening for autoimmune disease, or supporting mental health, the return on investment would be exponential. Healthy women lead. They innovate. They stabilize nations. They raise healthier children and build stronger economies. A woman in her fifties who stays healthy contributes more to her family, her workplace, and her community. She is a multiplier in every system she touches.

Women's health isn't a chapter in public health. It *is* public health.

The next time someone says "women's health," the image should not be a pregnant belly. It should be a twelve-year-old girl accessing vaccines, a thirty-five-year-old woman being screened for autoimmune disease, a fifty-five-year-old executive managing menopause without stigma, and a seventy-year-old grandmother walking without pain.

Because the health of women is the health of the world, and the world can't afford to ignore what women actually need.

Women's health isn't a chapter in public health. It *is* public health.

Chapter 3 Takeaways

- **WOMEN'S HEALTH EXTENDS FAR BEYOND REPRODUCTION.** THE LEADING CAUSES OF DEATH FOR WOMEN GLOBALLY ARE NON-COMMUNICABLE DISEASES LIKE HEART DISEASE, CANCER, AND STROKE—NOT PREGNANCY OR CHILDBIRTH.
- **HEALTH SYSTEMS STILL FOCUS ON FERTILITY WHILE NEGLECTING THE DECADES THAT FOLLOW.** CHRONIC DISEASE, AUTOIMMUNE DISORDERS, MENTAL HEALTH, AND MENOPAUSE REMAIN UNDERFUNDED AND UNDERPRIORITIZED.
- **WOMEN FACE A PERSISTENT DIAGNOSTIC GAP.** SYMPTOMS ARE MORE LIKELY TO BE DISMISSED, MISATTRIBUTED, OR DIAGNOSED LATER—DELAYING TREATMENT AND WORSENING OUTCOMES.
- **IGNORING WOMEN'S HEALTH ACROSS THE LIFESPAN CARRIES MASSIVE ECONOMIC COSTS.** CHRONIC DISEASE, UNTREATED MENTAL HEALTH, AND UNMANAGED MENOPAUSE REDUCE WORKFORCE PARTICIPATION, PRODUCTIVITY, AND LONG-TERM ECONOMIC STABILITY.

Chapter 4: The ROI

A global healthcare company, one that's been run by legacy family-owned leadership, was reviewing its pipeline. New leadership had just been brought on to "modernize" the company and expand the great product line the company already offers. A woman senior vice president proposed a new project focused on developing a diagnostic platform for cardiovascular disease in women. The science was promising—a breakthrough in detecting microvascular dysfunction (one of the most common and deadly forms of heart disease in women) was within reach.

After rigorous work, she put together and presented an entire business case. But when the financial modeling flashed across the screen, the male CFO didn't hesitate.

> *"Market too small. Let's cut it."*

The few women that were in the room were shocked when they heard this. I was shocked when I heard the story, but sadly not surprised. No one challenged the assumption. No one questioned the model. No one paused to ask whether the numbers reflected reality.

That meeting should have been inconsequential. Just another agenda item in a long line of operational decisions. But the consequences of that moment—like thousands of others happening quietly in corporate headquarters across the world—were anything but small.

The unmet market they dismissed wasn't "too small;" it was half the population. The lives affected were in the millions. The costs avoided were deferred losses that companies, governments, and societies will absorb for decades.

The pattern is repetitive, and I know because I've heard this story too many times, in too many rooms, to call it coincidence. Rational decisions are built on irrational models. Women's health is repeatedly deprioritized because the systems measuring value were never designed to see women fully in the first place.

And it shows: in GDP, in workforce participation, in healthcare costs, in innovation stagnation, and in the intergenerational loss of human capital. Ignoring women's health is an economic failure—a multitrillion-dollar one.

> Women's health is repeatedly deprioritized because the systems measuring value were never designed to see women fully in the first place.

Women make up half of the world's population. They drive 80 percent of consumer purchasing decisions in the healthcare industry, perform 75 percent of unpaid care work, and sustain entire communities through paid and invisible labor. Yet their health needs remain chronically underfunded and overlooked.

This disconnect isn't accidental. It's structural (see Chapter 2).

The Economic Blind Spot

Women's health is an investment strategy for the world's future, not a cost center. For decades, it was seen as a social issue or a moral imperative, but not an economic one. That assumption has cost the world trillions.

The global economy loses more every year to women's ill health than to war. The data are staggering:

- $400 billion in annual costs from lost productivity and preventable disease
- $12 trillion in potential GDP gains annually if gender gaps in health and work are closed

- A nine-time return on investment (ROI) in women's and children's health

In purely financial terms, the ROI in women's health outperforms nearly every other development strategy. No other sector in development or healthcare comes close to that multiplier. These aren't activist talking points. They come from the World Bank, McKinsey Global Institute, and the Global Financing Facility. The evidence is overwhelming: investing in women's health is one of the smartest economic decisions a nation or company can make.

Yet women's health receives less than 5 percent of biopharma research investment outside of oncology. Women remain underdiagnosed, misdiagnosed, untreated, excluded from trials, underserved by policy, and underfunded by investors. The result is predictable: lost productivity, preventable diseases, higher costs, and slower national growth.

> Ignoring women's health is economic malpractice.

Healthy women participate more fully in the workforce, lead more, invest more in their families and education, and drive community development. Unhealthy women withdraw from the workforce, from civic life, from leadership. And every preventable death or disability perpetuates cycles of poverty and dependency. Reproductive years are only one slice of that equation. Longevity, mental stability, and chronic disease prevention are the scaffolding of sustainable growth. Every untreated disease becomes a multiplier of lost potential.

Ignoring women's health is economic malpractice.

Women's Health as Infrastructure

We often think of "infrastructure" as roads, bridges, ports, water supply, power grids. These systems power economies and are the backbone of a nation. But in the twenty-first century, health—

particularly women's health—is infrastructure. It's the backbone of productivity, the foundation of human capital, and the driver of resilience and growth.

A bridge is useless if the people who build, teach, and maintain a community can't reach it because of illness. A digital economy can't thrive if half of its workforce is locked out by untreated depression or unmanaged menopause.

When women are healthy, economies expand. When women are ignored, economies shrink.

Governments measure GDP as industrial output, not human well-being. It tracks what people buy, not the inputs—energy, innovation, resilience—that actually keep society functioning and depend on human health. So it fails to capture unpaid care work, mental health, maternal health, social stability, workforce retention, preventive care ROI, and intergenerational gains.

This creates a distorted picture of economic health. Policymakers believe they're making rational decisions because the numbers appear logical. But when the numbers themselves are incomplete, every decision based on them is flawed.

This is simply arithmetic.

If you strip away politics, emotion, and outdated assumptions, what's left is a clean economic argument: the world loses extraordinary value—measured in trillions—because it refuses to treat women's health as central to growth. The numbers aren't abstract. They show up in workforce data, national budgets, stalled GDP, and household vulnerability. And the thread connecting each cost is simple: the systems making financial decisions are measured against the wrong baseline.

What gets measured gets funded. What gets ignored stays broken. As Allison Mignone, president of Mignone Family foundation and women's health philanthropist and investor, said at the 2026 Health of Women Investor Summit, "You can't improve what you can't measure." Women's health has never been measured accurately. That's why it has never been funded adequately.

Economies were built on the false belief that women's health is optional. But the losses incurred by that belief reveal the opposite: it is foundational.

Women's health is not a social program. It's hard infrastructure and every bit as essential as roads, power, and clean water. When it's seen through this lens, investment priorities change. It stops being a "soft" issue and becomes what it has always been: economic security.

Imagine what the GDP numbers could be if women were fully participating in the economy. That's the discussion economists should be having.

Visible Costs

When people cite the "$400 billion crisis," they're usually referring to the losses we can easily quantify. But even on its face, that number is jarring. Here are some examples that show up when you count it.

- Maternal mortality drains $15 billion annually from LMICs in lost productivity.
- Cardiovascular disease is projected to cost the global economy more than $1 trillion annually by 2030, with women facing higher rates of misdiagnosis and delayed care.
- Endometriosis affects one in ten women globally, with economic costs exceeding $70 billion each year.
- Migraine, which affects women three times more often than men, is a leading cause of disability worldwide, driving millions of lost workdays annually.
- Mental health conditions, especially depression and anxiety, which disproportionately affect women, cost the global economy $1 trillion every year.

These are the figures we can track. The ones we can model. The ones that fit into spreadsheets and annual reports.

Yet they tell only a fraction of the story.

Uncounted Costs

The real economic crisis is in the invisible losses. The world's largest subsidy isn't financial aid, agricultural support, or energy credits. It's unpaid care work, performed overwhelmingly by women.

Globally, women perform three-quarters of all unpaid care work caring for children, the sick, and the elderly. This work, if compensated, would account for 9 percent of global GDP—roughly $11 trillion a year. That's more than the entire tech sector and greater than the GDP of every country except the US and China.

In many parts of the world, when a woman falls sick, the consequences ripple far beyond the patient. In rural households across Africa and South Asia, it's often a daughter, not a son, who is pulled out of school to take over cooking and caring for younger siblings. The loss of a mother's health quickly becomes the loss of a girl's education and her future.

Healthy women stabilize entire economies.

The pattern is well documented. Studies across LMICs show that when a mother dies, girls are significantly more likely than boys to leave school to manage household responsibilities. Globally, girls already perform about 40 percent more unpaid care work than boys, and illness within the family deepens that imbalance.

Healthy women stabilize entire economies. When women have access to healthcare, families spend less on emergency care, children stay in school, and communities become more resilient. When women fall sick, that invisible labor force begins to collapse.

The economic consequences accumulate quickly. When girls leave school early, their lifetime earnings fall and workforce participation declines. The World Bank estimates that barriers preventing girls from completing secondary education cost the global economy between $15 to $30 trillion in lost lifetime productivity and earnings.

Yet because this labor happens inside homes rather than markets, it rarely appears in national budgets. Policymakers treat it as limitless and free.

This is macroeconomics.

Midlife Drop-Off

After childbirth, many women exit the workforce due to inadequate paid leave, mental health stigma, depression, physical recovery needs, childcare costs, or inflexible policies. Many never return. Those who do often return under immense stress.

If women everywhere took a single day off from unpaid care work, economies would collapse. And if economists counted this work correctly, women's health would immediately become a national priority because it's the foundation on which everything else stands.

Countries, such as Norway and Rwanda, with strong maternal health support, affordable childcare, and flexible workplace policies have higher female workforce participation, higher fertility rates, lower healthcare costs, and faster GDP growth.

Meanwhile, women in their forties and fifties are some of the most experienced, highest-performing, and influential leaders in organizations. They also represent the demographic most impacted by unmanaged chronic conditions and perimenopause symptoms like fatigue, sleep disruption, cognitive fog, pain, and anxiety.

A 2023 Deloitte survey showed that one in five women have left a job due to insufficient menopause support, and 30 percent have considered leaving for the same reason.

It's the ill-fated cost of pretending women's health is a "personal issue" rather than a business one.

Companies rarely connect the dots. They track turnover. They track productivity dips. They track engagement declines. But they rarely ask why women leave or why performance suffers.

The answer isn't mysterious. Women in midlife are often dealing with:

- Perimenopause and menopause symptoms
- Aging parents requiring care
- Teenagers needing guidance
- Career peak responsibilities
- Chronic health issues diagnosed later than men

These pressures converge at the exact moment women are poised to move into the highest-impact leadership roles.

A 2023 Mayo Clinic study estimated that menopause-related productivity losses cost US companies $26 billion annually. In the UK, the number exceeds £10 billion annually. The figure is likely much higher globally, yet almost no employers track it.

Ignoring this is a talent leak of historic proportions.

The equation is straightforward: supporting women during all of their productive years is one of the highest-return policy decisions any nation can make.

Returns on Investment

The most compelling case for investing in women's health isn't the moral one; it's the economic one. And that case has three pillars.

1. DIRECT PRODUCTIVITY RETURNS

Companies talk endlessly about the lack of women in senior leadership. They usually frame it as a "pipeline problem" when it's actually a health and support problem. Healthier women work more hours, miss fewer days, require less costly medical intervention, stay in the workforce longer, progress further in their careers, and generate more income and tax revenue.

Companies have more to gain from women's health investments than any other stakeholder:

- Higher retention
- Lower turnover costs
- Increased leadership diversity
- Higher innovation output
- More resilient teams
- Stronger employer brand

A workforce that feels supported performs better. Period.

When companies ignore women's health, they pay the price in lost institutional knowledge and leadership attrition. When they invest in women's health, they outperform.

THE RETURN ON **INCLUSION**

Investment Area	Estimate	Source
Women's & children's health	9x ROI	*The Lancet*
Cervical cancer elimination	3.2:1 ROI	WHO
Family planning	$120B savings annually	UNFPA
Gender equity in workforce	$12T added to global GDP	McKinsey
Mental health parity	4:1 ROI	WHO
Osteoporosis prevention	50% reduction in disability costs	IOF

This is an operational strategy, not a "DEI initiative."

Companies that lead on women's health will define the talent markets of the next decade and the global markets of the ones that follow. Every country battling labor shortages should start here.

2. PREVENTIVE COST SAVINGS

When women receive preventive care—family planning, mental health support, vaccinations, general health screenings, and cardiovascular screening—societies avoid:

- Emergency care spending
- Chronic disease management
- Maternal complications
- Preterm birth costs
- Untreated mental health crises

The cost difference between prevention and intervention can be staggering. The HPV vaccine, for example, can cost as little as \$4-\$13 per dose through global procurement programs, yet treating advanced cervical cancer can range from \$10,000-\$40,000 per patient, not including the long-term economic impact of lost productivity and caregiving burdens.

When a \$10 vaccine can prevent a \$40,000 cancer, the question is no longer whether prevention works. The question becomes why do health systems continue to fund the consequences instead of the infrastructure that prevents them.

3. INTERGENERATIONAL RETURNS

Here's where the numbers explode: when women's health deteriorates, the decline doesn't stay confined to one person. It ripples outward and forward. When a woman dies in childbirth, her children are more likely to drop out of school, experience poor health, and live in poverty. When a mother's health suffers, children's nutrition suffers. When a girl misses school due to menstruation stigma or untreated illness, her earning potential diminishes. When women exit the workforce, future tax revenues decline and poverty rises.

These are predictable economic outcomes with predictable

generational effects. And the global evidence is consistent:

- Investing in maternal and reproductive health can yield returns of up to twenty-five to one when intergenerational outcomes are included. She invests in her children, they produce higher future income, and the cycle compounds.
- Countries that improve women's health see faster reductions in poverty and stronger long-term growth.
- Every additional year of a girl's education increases her future income by 10 to 20 percent.

The fastest-growing economies of the last half-century have one thing in common: improving women's health and education early in their development curves. If you want to understand the future of a country, look at the health of its women. That's the leading indicator.

It's economics, not a coincidence.

> If you want to understand the future of a country, look at the health of its women.

Innovation Gap

For decades, global health innovation revolved around infectious diseases and maternal health. Despite women driving 80 percent of consumer purchasing decisions in the healthcare industry, the majority of health innovations—drugs, devices, AI models, diagnostics—are still designed through a male default lens.

It's bad business, and it's biased.

Today, a new generation of innovators—scientists, entrepreneurs, clinicians, and engineers—are broadening that focus to include the full spectrum of women's lives.

FemTech, a once-niche category popularized by entrepreneur

Ida Tin, has exploded into a multibillion-dollar industry and catalyzed a cultural and investment shift. Depending on whose forecast you trust, the global FemTech market is projected to reach between $26 and $117 billion by the end of the decade. Allied Market Research downgraded its outlook in 2024, citing operational, funding, and regulatory challenges. Even the most optimistic projection is roughly one-tenth of the $1 trillion women's health gap McKinsey identified. The infrastructure isn't there to capture the opportunity. As awareness, capital, and demographic shifts accelerate, women's health will become one of the dominant fields in medtech, biotech, and digital health.

Younger researchers, entrepreneurs, and innovators are building a new definition of women's health—one that spans the lifetime, incorporates lived experience, and integrates physical, mental, and economic well-being. What began as apps for fertility tracking has evolved into a robust ecosystem tackling menopause, endometriosis, chronic pain, and sexual health. Startups are developing digital therapeutics for postpartum depression, portable diagnostics for cervical screening, and wearable sensors for hormonal monitoring. Innovation is starting to meet reality.

Recent studies in *The Lancet Regional Health – Americas* and from the Royal College of Obstetricians & Gynaecologists outline research priorities that finally align with women's real burden of disease: autoimmune conditions, cardiovascular health, bone health, mental health, and sex-specific drug interactions. These are central to human progress, not fringe issues.

The question isn't whether we can broaden the definition of women's health. It's whether we will.

As Jessica Federer, managing director of the Women's Health Fund said at the March 2026 Health of Women Investor Summit: "Women's health is the category with the most opportunity for scientific and economic advancement in our lifetimes."

Investors who dismiss women's health as a niche are ignoring the largest underdeveloped segment in the global health economy. The companies that correct this blind spot will lead the next wave of health innovation and become wealthy as a result. Women's health is no longer an afterthought; it's a growth sector.

WHAT HAPPENS WHEN WE FINALLY **INVEST IN WOMEN'S HEALTH?**

When women are healthy, the entire economic architecture stabilizes.

- **WE SEE HIGHER WORKFORCE PARTICIPATION.** COUNTRIES WITH STRONG MATERNAL HEALTH PROGRAMS AND CHILDCARE SUPPORT HAVE MORE WOMEN WORKING, AND MORE WOMEN LEADING.
- **WE SEE STRONGER GDP GROWTH.** RWANDA, VIETNAM, ICELAND, AND SOUTH KOREA ALL DEMONSTRATE HOW WOMEN'S HEALTH INVESTMENTS SHIFT NATIONAL TRAJECTORIES.
- **WE SEE GREATER RESILIENCE.** COMMUNITIES WITH HEALTHIER WOMEN RECOVER FASTER FROM CRISES.
- **WE SEE INNOVATION ACCELERATE.** DIVERSE R&D PIPELINES AND INCLUSIVE DESIGN LEAD TO BREAKTHROUGHS THAT BENEFIT EVERYONE.
- **WE SEE GENERATIONAL CHANGE.** HEALTHIER MOTHERS RAISE HEALTHIER, MORE EDUCATED CHILDREN WHO CONTRIBUTE MORE TO SOCIETY.

The transformation doesn't take generations. It takes strategy.

The Shift from Burden to Blueprint

For centuries, women were framed as dependents and recipients of care, not drivers of growth. But data tells the opposite story. Women's health is the blueprint for national prosperity.

The economic consequences are massive when women are not healthy:

- Families lose income.
- Companies lose talent and pay to replace it.
- Governments lose tax revenue.
- Children experience downstream impacts in education and well-being.
- GDP shrinks due to lower labor participation.

None of this is inevitable.

Countries that prioritize women's health, like Rwanda and South Korea, have stronger GDP, more stable workforces, healthier families, and more resilient communities. This isn't due to cultural norms or shifts. This is because women's health is treated as structural and part of the fabric of their society.

It's the difference between treating women's health as charity and treating it as a strategy.

> Women's health is the blueprint for national prosperity.

For decades, women's health has been approached as an expense category—another budget line that leaders, like the CFO at the global healthcare company I told you about earlier, try to minimize. But treating women's health as a cost center is a category error. It misunderstands what health investment actually is: the engine of productivity, the stabilizer of societies, and the hidden architecture beneath every strong economy.

Once you shift the frame from "cost" to "infrastructure," everything changes. The logic becomes clear, the returns become obvious, and the old assumptions collapse under their own inefficiency.

The question that transforms this entire narrative is simple: what happens when we stop ignoring women and start investing in them?

The answer: economies grow—faster, fairer, and more sustainably.

We are no longer in a theoretical planning phase. It's a measurable, documented reality. And the transformation takes infrastructure.

Chapter 4 Takeaways

- **IGNORING WOMEN'S HEALTH IS A MULTI-TRILLION-DOLLAR ECONOMIC FAILURE.** LOST PRODUCTIVITY, PREVENTABLE DISEASE, AND WORKFORCE ATTRITION MAKE UNDERINVESTMENT IN WOMEN'S HEALTH ECONOMICALLY IRRATIONAL.
- **WOMEN'S HEALTH IS HARD INFRASTRUCTURE, NOT A SIDE ISSUE.** IT UNDERPINS LABOR FORCE PARTICIPATION, HUMAN CAPITAL, RESILIENCE, AND LONG-TERM GDP GROWTH.
- **WHAT ISN'T MEASURED IN WOMEN'S HEALTH DOESN'T GET FUNDED.** ECONOMIES STILL IGNORE UNPAID CARE WORK, MIDLIFE HEALTH, PREVENTION, AND INTERGENERATIONAL RETURNS, DISTORTING CAPITAL ALLOCATION AT SCALE.
- **INVESTING IN WOMEN'S HEALTH IS ONE OF THE HIGHEST-RETURN GROWTH STRATEGIES AVAILABLE.** THE UPSIDE SHOWS UP IN RETENTION, PRODUCTIVITY, LOWER HEALTHCARE COSTS, STRONGER FAMILIES, AND FASTER, MORE DURABLE ECONOMIC GROWTH.

PART II: THE FRAMEWORK

We often mistake innovation for technology—a device, an app, or a platform. But true innovation is much broader: it's structural, cultural, and economic. It's about the conditions that make new ideas possible and sustainable.

Technology can amplify change, but it can't substitute for it. A brilliant app will fail in an ecosystem that doesn't support its users. A diagnostic device is useless if the women who need it can't afford or access it. A data algorithm trained on male-dominant datasets will reproduce bias at scale.

Take telehealth. It's one of the most cited examples of progress in access, and for good reason: it can collapse geography, remove travel costs, and connect patients to clinicians across borders. Yet without equity built in, it can deepen exclusion. Women in low- and middle-income countries are 17 percent less likely than men to own a smartphone and 19 percent less likely to use mobile internet, limiting their ability to access telehealth services as healthcare systems digitize. In high-income countries, women with caregiving responsibilities may lack privacy or time to use digital care effectively. Unless we address that digital divide through affordable connectivity, device access, and digital literacy, telehealth can easily become a mirror of inequity rather than a solution to it.

The same holds true for AI diagnostics, wearables, and remote-monitoring tools.

But innovation doesn't always mean developing a new technology or product for the market. Innovation also looks like new (or even old and repurposed) business models.

Every year, hospitals in wealthy nations discard high-value, functioning medical equipment (diagnostic imaging systems, monitors, surgical tools) simply because replacement cycles and warranties demand "new." It's perfectly serviceable technology that becomes waste, just like the mammography machine that I figured out how to deliver to a remote clinic in Costa Rica.

That whole experience led me to found HERhealthEQ, a nonprofit that intercepts that usable "waste" stream, refurbishes it, and redistributes it to hospitals and clinics serving women in LMICs. A mammography unit retired in New York can extend its life by more than a decade in a Latin American clinic, enabling tens of thousands of screenings. Each repurposed device adds diagnostic capacity, trains clinicians, and prevents tons of electronic waste.

> True innovation is structural, cultural, and economic.

But we don't just shove products at the healthcare providers in LMICs. We ask them what they need. We focus on the specific equipment that serves the needs of the people on the ground doing the work. We provide training and service and maintenance contracts. With support, local doctors, nurses, and midwives can deploy accessible healthcare in the way they know how with better technologies.

Within the first decade of operating, we've deployed more than sixty pieces of equipment and improved the health outcomes of more than 135,000 women across twelve different LMICs. This means health systems can finally diagnose instead of just managing symptoms, resulting in early cancer detection and reduced mortality.

HERhealthEQ is proof that innovation isn't just about what's new. It's about right-sized solutions that are sustainable. After more than a decade of building and trialing different frameworks and methods, I can now name what made it work.

The Architecture of Innovation

Innovation that lasts is built, not improvised. It requires structure—

the scaffolding that turns creative ideas into scalable change. The architecture of innovation in women's health rests on five pillars: research, funding, policy, partnership, and people.

1. RESEARCH: SEEING THE WHOLE PICTURE

Data is destiny. When research excludes women, innovation inherits that bias. Devices, drugs, and diagnostics calibrated to male physiology often fail female patients or delay accurate diagnosis. The solution isn't simply "include women." It's to redesign research from the ground up, requiring sex-disaggregated data, life-course analysis, and intersectional sampling that captures differences across race, age, and environment.

Data equity is the foundation of every other kind of equity. Without it, we're just guessing.

2. FUNDING: REDEFINING VALUE

Money determines momentum. What gets financed gets built. Historically, women's health has been dismissed as "niche" or "non-scalable."

Venture funding for women-led startups remains in the single digits, and only a fraction of global development aid targets women's health directly. But new patterns are emerging: gender-lens investing, blended-finance models, micro-venture networks, and corporate venture arms dedicated to health equity. These mechanisms treat women's health as both a social priority and an economic engine.

It's been mentioned before, but it's important: closing gender gaps in health and employment could add $12 trillion to global GDP. That's a market signal.

3. POLICY: TURNING MOMENTUM INTO MANDATE

Policy is the quiet engine of innovation. It defines what counts as essential care, who pays for it, and how fast it scales. Without policy, innovation depends on philanthropy and luck; with it, change becomes systemic.

Gender-sensitive policy is the operating system of equitable healthcare. Legislation that mandates inclusion in clinical research, coverage for maternal and reproductive services, or incentives for health-equity innovation changes the playing field permanently. Good policy translates intention into infrastructure.

4. PARTNERSHIP: BREAKING DOWN SILOS

No single sector can solve women's health. Governments control scale, corporations control capital, NGOs control trust, and communities control context. The future belongs to those who combine them. Cross-sector collaboration—public-private partnerships, academic-industry alliances, NGO-corporate hybrids—has proven it can move faster than traditional hierarchies.

Partnership turns isolated pilots into sustainable systems.

> Innovation without representation is theory. With it, it becomes reality.

5. PEOPLE: THE HUMAN ENGINE

At its core, innovation is human. Women comprise 70 percent of the global health workforce but occupy only 25 percent of leadership roles. That imbalance isn't a pipeline problem; it's a power problem.

When leadership tables lack women, entire categories of need remain invisible. Innovation slows because imagination narrows. As Justice Ruth Bader Ginsburg said, "Women should be in all the places where decisions are being made." Until they are, health systems will continue to overlook half their stakeholders.

Innovation without representation is theory. With it, it becomes reality.

Beyond the Binary

The premise of this book is not up for debate: women's health is infrastructure, the status quo has a measurable cost, and inaction is a choice with consequences.

The architecture of innovation is a framework based on my

twenty-five years of working inside the system. It reflects what I've seen succeed and what I've watched fail across four continents, in boardrooms and clinics and government offices and startup pitches that went nowhere. I believe in it. But no single perspective captures the whole picture. If you've taken a different approach and achieved results, that perspective matters. Progress in women's health has always come from people testing ideas, sharing what works, and building on each other's experience.

This framework is meant to open the conversation. Think of it as a starting point, not a prescription. It would be hypocritical to write a book about co-creation and then hand you a model you're not allowed to touch.

Frameworks only become valuable when people use them—when they adapt them, test them, improve them, and bring what they learn back to the table.

That's how systems evolve. It's how infrastructure gets built.

If this framework helps you see a new path or build something better, then it has done its job. And if it does, I'd love to hear what you learn.

Chapter 5: **Design Differently**

Innovation breaks down when it's built on narrow assumptions. And for most of modern healthcare, the foundational assumption has been that the male body is the default. Companies rarely call it that, but the results are obvious: devices that don't fit women's hands, drugs calibrated to male metabolism, algorithms trained on male-dominant datasets, and clinical trials that treat women as optional. These aren't accidents; they're legacies—and they're a starting point for rebuilding.

What's misunderstood is how simple the fix is. Designing for women isn't complicated, expensive, or disruptive. It doesn't add years to development timelines. It doesn't require specialized teams tucked off in a corner working on "women's versions" of products. It requires something far more basic: put women in the room, listen to them, test with them, and let their insights shape the product before it's locked in. That's it. And yet, this straightforward approach is still treated as advanced practice in many organizations.

Innovation always reflects the people creating it. Teams made up of one demographic, regardless of which demographic, produce blind spots. They see a narrow slice of the world and assume it's universal. When women aren't part of early scoping, problem identification skews. When women aren't in engineering discussions, design constraints ignore entire categories of users. When women aren't included in clinical trials, safety profiles are incomplete. When women aren't present in leadership, the wrong trade-offs get prioritized.

No amount of good intention overrides structural absence.

The most dangerous assumption companies make is that if a product works "well enough" for men, it will work well enough for women. The same holds true for HIC versus LMIC design thinking. Those assumptions are responsible for a century of design failures.

Consider orthopedic instruments built around the average male grip. A physician and senior medtech executive told me about an experience she had early in her career when she worked at one of the largest surgical equipment manufacturers. During a visit with R&D, she tried to grasp the equipment they were creating, but she couldn't easily. The team leader told her the equipment wasn't the issue, that she should try harder or get stronger. This is an industry-wide issue I've seen and heard about with other medical equipment manufacturers.

Female orthopedic surgeons account for less than 10 percent of the global surgical workforce and are using tools that strain their hands, alter their technique, and impact precision. But they're not the only ones impacted by the tools' poor design. Among all surgeons, 87 percent reported musculoskeletal pain, with ergonomic design cited as a major contributor. Female surgeons reported higher ergonomic mismatch. That's a safety and performance issue, not a preference issue—and it's entirely avoidable.

The same problem exists in software and diagnostics. AI systems are only as good as the data they learn from, and much of that data reflects decades of male-centered medical research. When algorithms are trained on skewed datasets, they can replicate the same blind spots that are already present in healthcare.

No amount of good intention overrides structural absence.

The gaps are measurable. One landmark study found that commercial AI systems had error rates under 1 percent for light-skinned men but as high as 34.7 percent for darker-skinned women, revealing how demographic imbalance in training data can produce dramatically different outcomes. Similar patterns are emerging in clinical tools. Researchers have shown that medical imaging algorithms trained on gender-imbalanced datasets perform significantly worse for female patients.

When datasets reflect only part of the population, algorithms learn only part of the truth. When development teams don't question the data feeding their models, they hardwire inequity into the product. And once inequity is coded in, it's incredibly difficult and costly to remove.

Look at medical devices used only on women. Mammography machines were designed decades ago with almost no consideration for the experience of the person using them. If men had been the primary users, the devices would have been redesigned long ago. The same is true for the vaginal speculum. A century-old design remained untouched not because better engineering was impossible but because women's discomfort wasn't treated as an innovation opportunity. Only when women-led teams prioritized user experience did meaningful redesigns emerge.

It begins with how problems are defined. When women are part of that initial framing, the scope expands. The definition of success expands. The choices about what gets prioritized expand. Better framing leads to better innovation.

Here's where diverse voices matter most: upstream. By the time a company gets to prototyping or clinical trial stages, the cost of correcting biased assumptions skyrockets. But if women shape the thinking from the first meeting, the entire pipeline changes. That's why representation in early-stage product strategy—not just final testing—is non-negotiable.

> Design is the silent architecture of inequity and the most powerful tool for change.

When companies commit to this, the quality of innovation jumps quickly. Women notice things others overlook: the ergonomics of a device, the practicality of a workflow, the pain points baked into a process, the unintended consequences of a design detail. Not because women are inherently better at noticing these things, but because their lived experience is different. And innovation relies on different.

When you line up perspectives that differ, performance improves. Companies build better products because they understand their users more deeply. They enter new markets more confidently. They avoid costly redesigns caused by missing voices.

Design is the silent architecture of inequity and the most powerful tool for change.

Every rule, process, and policy was designed by someone. Re-engineering women's health begins with re-engineering design itself. Designing for what's next requires three shifts: from reactive to proactive, from generic to contextual, and from incremental to systemic

1. FROM REACTIVE TO PROACTIVE

Historically, healthcare systems have been reactive—waiting for illness to appear, for data to emerge, for crises to demand attention. But innovation thrives in anticipation.

Proactive design means building systems that predict needs rather than simply respond to them.

That's where technology, policy, and public health must align. Predictive analytics, population health models, preventive health programs, and community-based preventive care can transform outcomes, but only when they're inclusive. For women, this means designing early-detection tools that account for sex-based biological differences, culturally sensitive education programs, prevention programs that are inclusive and right-sized, and health financing systems that don't penalize motherhood or age.

A proactive system doesn't wait for women to fall through the cracks; it redesigns the floor.

2. FROM GENERIC TO CONTEXTUAL

Global health has too often defaulted to one-size-fits-all models developed in high-income countries and exported elsewhere. But what works in Boston won't necessarily work in Bogotá or Bangalore. Innovation must be context-aware.

The most effective solutions are localized—built from the inside out, not imposed from the top down. It means designing with, not for, communities. It means funding local researchers and innovators who understand the nuanced intersection of gender, culture, and economy in their regions.

Contextual design asks a simple but revolutionary question: who will use this, and under what conditions?

From there, innovation becomes practical, not paternalistic.

3. FROM INCREMENTAL TO SYSTEMIC

Incrementalism is safe. It tweaks the edges but leaves the core intact. Systemic innovation, by contrast, reconfigures power.

That's the shift women's health now demands.

We can't simply add new programs or products. We must rewire how systems define value, measure success, and allocate resources. When innovation becomes systemic, it stops being dependent on champions and becomes embedded policy.

That's what separates a pilot project from a paradigm shift. Constraint is where the most durable design shifts have happened, which is why it's worth understanding how limitation produces innovation rather than preventing it.

From Constraint Comes Creativity

Every breakthrough in global health has been born of limitation.

Smallpox eradication started with scarcity of vaccines and personnel. Telemedicine emerged from isolation and lack of clinicians. Portable ultrasound devices were created not in abundance but in absence. Constraint is the catalyst of innovation, not the enemy.

Women's health has lived within constraint for generations. In that vacuum, women have always innovated informally: community midwives delivering babies where hospitals wouldn't; mothers sharing home remedies where clinics were out of reach; scientists and entrepreneurs launching companies after personal experiences with neglect or misdiagnosis. What looks like scarcity on paper often hides enormous creative capacity.

Constraint incubates clarity.

It forces prioritization. It asks: what matters most?

That's where we are now. Women's health innovation is no longer a fringe conversation; it's a global imperative. When traditional models fail, people start building new ones. Across every region, innovators are reimagining how care is financed, delivered, and measured with women at the center rather than the margins.

This is recognition that pressure creates progress, not optimism for its own sake.

But innovation reflects the people who were and were not in the room. If the data is biased, the algorithm will be biased. If the testing population is narrow, performance will be narrow. If the design assumes privilege—private phone access, reliable electricity, broadband, literacy, time, safety—then anyone outside those conditions is quietly excluded.

That's the difference between equality and equity and confusing the two is how technology becomes another barrier.

Equity vs. Equality

Equality is seductive because it sounds fair: same services, same products, same access for everyone. But equality assumes everyone begins at the same starting point. They don't, and they never have.

Equality says: give them the same tool.

Equity asks: what does each woman need for this tool to work in her actual life?

Equality is not equity, and confusing the two is exactly how technology becomes another barrier instead of a breakthrough.

A few examples make the point:

- The woman in rural Kenya without a personal phone isn't starting where the woman in Seattle with unlimited data is.
- The domestic worker in São Paulo who can't miss a day of work isn't starting where the consultant in Toronto working remotely is.
- The adolescent girl in northern India facing child marriage doesn't navigate care like the university student in Melbourne.
- The woman experiencing intimate partner violence in London cannot safely use most digital health apps, no matter how "accessible" they claim to be.

The tech trap appears when innovation is deployed into health systems without addressing the underlying social, cultural, or environmental barriers that shape women's lives. It appears when solutions assume literacy in the language used, access to consistent electricity or data, personal phone ownership, privacy within the household, Global North-trained datasets, safe domestic relationships, free time to engage with care, stable identification and documentation, and a basic level of agency that billions of women simply do not have.

It's the assumption that technology is inherently fair, scalable, and accessible. Unfortunately, it's not. When these assumptions go unchallenged, technology accelerates access for the already served and widens the gap for everyone else.

Equity cannot be a publicity line, donor requirement, late-stage review, marketing exercise, "version 2.0" patch, or an afterthought. Equity must be part of the architecture. It must shape the first brainstorming session, the earliest prototypes, the data strategy, the clinical validation, the language choices, and the rollout plan.

Equity is design realism and the blueprint for scale. Innovation doesn't scale equitably unless equity is intentionally designed into it.

Build for the Edges, Not the Center

Design teams love the "average user." It's efficient, predictable, and easy. But in practice, the "average user" always resembles the people doing the designing: urban, educated, digitally literate, relatively privileged.

Healthcare has no "average user."

It has human beings with diverse bodies, cultures, power dynamics, risks, and constraints.

When you design only for the easiest user, you miss the real barriers women face, misjudge your market, reinforce distrust in health institutions, build products that collapse as soon as they leave the ideal environment, and guarantee inequity at scale. When you design for the "average user," you design for almost no one.

Women are not part of the edge. Neither are people of color, rural communities, migrants, LGBTQ+ women, or low-income households. Yet the industry still treats them as fringe cases. If the people building the solution don't reflect the people meant to use it, the product will fail the moment it encounters real diversity. We've seen it play out again and again.

> If the people building the solution don't reflect the people meant to use it, the product will fail the moment it encounters real diversity.

For decades, healthcare technologies—from pulse oximeters to AI diagnostic systems—were designed and trained on narrow populations, producing tools that worked well for some patients while quietly failing millions of others. Most of those high-profile failures (listed in the sidebar on p. 73) weren't caused by technological limitations. They were caused by voluntary blindness. Teams chose speed over inclusion, homogeneity over representation, assumptions over inquiry, convenience over context, or efficiency over humanity.

Communities reject technology because it doesn't fit their lives, not because they're "resistant." Innovation is slow, human, contextual work, and nowhere is that more obvious than in women's health.

Designing for the edges expands your market. It's how good innovation becomes scalable innovation. Successful programs that design with intended users (like a new vaginal speculum design or self-collection swabs that allow for cultural sensitivity) flip the typical design approach. Instead of designing for the "easiest user" and retrofitting later, design for the person with the most constraints.

Design for the woman with low literacy, limited privacy, irregular income, complex family dynamics, long travel distances, or unpredictable work schedules. Design for the woman facing partner violence, the migrant worker with employer-controlled mobility, or the mother without electricity or a smartphone. Design for the transgender woman repeatedly dismissed by the system, the grandmother caring for multiple dependents, or the woman facing stigma around HIV or infertility.

It's superior engineering, not idealism. If your solution works for her, it will work for everyone else. When it doesn't work for her, it's a product problem. The same mistakes still repeat today, not because we can't fix them, but because too many organizations still choose not to.

Designing for the center leads to brittle innovation that only works under ideal conditions. But tech that starts at the margins becomes stronger, more adaptable, and more universal. Here's the shift happening now: the most inclusive technologies are becoming the most formidable technologies.

The world isn't short on innovation; it's short on equitable innovation.

Companies that understand this will lead the next decade. Those that ignore it will watch their relevance fade. The competitive edge is shifting from technical sophistication to contextual intelligence. The innovations that will reshape global women's health won't be the flashiest. They'll be the ones that understand women's real lives, especially the lives of women farthest from power.

If you want to see the future of healthcare, don't look at the center. The future is being built at the edges.

Co-Creating with Healthcare Workers

My years spent observing programs across Africa, Latin America, South Asia, and underserved areas of the US made one point unavoidable: technology succeeds only when the community sees value and ownership.

Here's what consistently separates long-lasting, high-impact innovations from the ones that die immediately after the pilot.

1. COMMUNITIES HELP DEFINE THE PROBLEM

Most tech failures begin with a wrong diagnosis of the problem. An innovation team decides "pregnant women need appointment reminders," when the real barrier is transportation costs, gender norms, or facility disrespect. A telehealth strategy assumes virtual visits will increase access, when the real issue is that women can't safely speak on the phone at home.

If you solve the wrong problem, it doesn't matter how elegant your solution is.

2. HEALTH WORKERS MUST BENEFIT

Women make up the backbone of global health delivery, especially in low-resource settings. If technology adds time, increases reporting

FAILED PRODUCTS BUILT FOR THE "AVERAGE USER"

What is the average user? When products are built for the previous design standard of a white male, they miss the populations they might be serving most.

- **PULSE OXIMETERS CALIBRATED ON LIGHTER SKIN.** OXYGEN LEVELS ARE READ INACCURATELY IN PEOPLE WITH DARKER SKIN BECAUSE THE DEVICE WAS CALIBRATED ALMOST EXCLUSIVELY ON LIGHTER-SKINNED BODIES. THE RESULT: MILLIONS OF PEOPLE RECEIVED DELAYED OR INADEQUATE CARE.
- **APPLE HEALTH LAUNCH WITHOUT MENSTRUAL TRACKING.** A PLATFORM THAT COULD TRACK CHROMIUM FORGOT MENSTRUATION COMPLETELY. THIS WAS A DESIGN CULTURE PROBLEM.
- **AI DERMATOLOGY TOOLS TRAINED ON LIGHT SKIN.** MULTIPLE APPS DRAMATICALLY UNDERPERFORMED ON DARKER SKIN BECAUSE THE TRAINING DATASETS WEREN'T DIVERSE. "DEMOCRATIZING ACCESS" BACKFIRED.
- **TELEHEALTH INTERFACES IN ENGLISH ONLY.** DURING THE PANDEMIC, MAJOR US PLATFORMS EXCLUDED IMMIGRANTS AND NON-ENGLISH SPEAKERS—PRECISELY THE PEOPLE WHO NEEDED REMOTE CARE THE MOST.
- **MATERNAL HEALTH APPS ASSUMING PHONE OWNERSHIP.** IN MANY REGIONS, PHONE ACCESS IS CONTROLLED BY HUSBANDS. PROGRAMS THAT REQUIRED PRIVATE PHONES NEVER REACHED THE WOMEN THEY INTENDED TO SERVE.

- **HPV VACCINES NOT REACHING GIRLS IN LMICS.** AUSTRALIA IS ON TRACK TO ELIMINATE CERVICAL CANCER BY 2035. MEANWHILE, GIRLS IN LMICS REMAIN UNVACCINATED DUE TO PRICE, SUPPLY, AND SYSTEM GAPS. EQUITY IS THE BARRIER, NOT INNOVATION.
- **WEARABLES INACCURATE FOR WOMEN AND LARGER BODIES.** STEP COUNTS, HEART RATES, EVEN SLEEP METRICS WERE CALIBRATED ON MALE PHYSIOLOGY. THE TOOLS "FOR EVERYONE" WERE NEVER ACTUALLY TESTED ON EVERYONE.

None of these failures required new science to prevent. They required inclusion.

burdens, or feels like surveillance, adoption evaporates.

When tools genuinely make frontline work easier, workers advocate for them.

3. TRAINING AND SUPPORT MATTER MORE THAN SOFTWARE

Tech itself is rarely the barrier. Scale depends on consistent training, ongoing mentorship, clear incentives, integration with existing workflows, and government alignment.

Software is easy. Human systems are the hard part.

4. REAL-WORLD CONDITIONS SHAPE SUCCESS

If a tool breaks without reliable electricity, fails with spotty connectivity, or requires individual logins in settings where ID systems don't exist, it dies on arrival. That's a design failure.

The best innovations assume nothing and test everything.

Neopenda's neonatal vital signs monitor is a masterclass in co-creation.

I first met this company in 2021 when I was serving as a venture partner for a fund investing in African healthcare solutions. I performed diligence and suggested investment by the fund. I've been following Neopenda's evolution ever since, through product iterations, business model shifts, and growing impact.

In overcrowded neonatal wards, the biggest danger isn't the illness. It's the silence. When the nurse-to-patient ratios make continuous monitoring impossible, vital signs often go unheard. Not because of a lack of technology, but because there aren't enough people to monitor vital signs across multiple screens.

Sona Shah co-founded Neopenda with one clear goal: to ensure every patient, no matter where they're born, has a fair shot at a healthy life. The idea was born from Shah's work in biomedical engineering at Columbia University and firsthand experience in Kenya, where she witnessed significant healthcare inequities, like the gap between what neonatal care could look like and how it actually looked in understaffed facilities.

Unlike many "frugal innovation" attempts, Neopenda didn't strip down a Western device and call it accessible. The company built a new model grounded in context. The neoGuard—a wearable, low-cost sensor that monitors essential vitals for newborns—was co-created with Ugandan clinicians and designed specifically for understaffed and low-resource hospital environments. Workflows reflect actual practice, not Western textbook standards. It was built prioritizing equity.

From 2015 to 2021, Neopenda built and refined the neonatal monitoring device with nurses in Ugandan hospitals. Early prototypes were redesigned based on frontline feedback about alarm fatigue, usability, and workflow—an example of designing with clinicians rather than for them. The result is a product that doesn't just arrive at the hospital and get locked in a closet. It stays at the bedside and does the work it was built to do.

The neoGuard succeeds because every decision was shaped by real constraints: it's resilient to electricity instability (low-power and durable), built for the real nurse-to-baby ratios (one dashboard monitoring multiple infants), priced with realistic procurement and maintenance pathways, and includes training as central to the system.

The co-creation of this device translates to 4,500 infants whose vitals were tracked (150,000 hours of continuous monitoring) by the technology when a nurse was busy in another corner of the ward. That's 4,500 lives that had a better chance of recovery and returning home because a change in heart rate or oxygen saturation was caught in time.

Neopenda demonstrates that designing for constraints is an accelerator for scale.

Trust grows when technology consistently meets women's needs while respecting their realities.

Designing for Trust: The Four Pillars

If there is one universal truth in global health innovation, it's this:

nothing works without trust. You can deploy the most elegant solution in the world, but if the women using it don't trust the system, the clinician, the company, or the technology itself, the chances of sustained adoption are near zero.

Trust is not a user experience feature. It's not a marketing layer. It's not something you add once the product is finished. Trust is built or lost through every design choice.

Trust grows when technology consistently meets women's needs while respecting their realities.

Four pillars shape that experience.

1. SAFETY

Physical, social, emotional, and digital safety is non-negotiable. Women need assurance that a product will not expose them to harm, whether it's through messages that can be seen by controlling partners, data that can be traced or misused, notifications that reveal sensitive conditions, or content that triggers stigma or danger.

A "helpful" feature in one setting may be a liability in another. Safety must be the first design question, not a late-stage consideration.

2. RESPECT

Women engage with technologies that treat them as partners, not passive recipients. Respect shows up in culturally appropriate language, non-judgmental framing, acknowledgment of lived realities, and inclusive design across identities.

If a product talks down to women or assumes incompetence, it won't matter how powerful the underlying technology is.

3. COMPETENCE

Reliability builds trust. Unreliable tools destroy it instantly. Women will not repeatedly use devices that misread vitals, apps that freeze, alerts that trigger false alarms, results that contradict clinicians, or interfaces that break in low-connectivity areas.

Competence is about performance in real conditions.

4. RELATABILITY

A solution must feel relevant to women's lives. A product designed around Western work schedules or nuclear-family structures will never resonate globally. Relatability builds emotional trust: "This was built with someone like me in mind."

Tools that ignore women's lived experience are forgettable. Tools that acknowledge it become indispensable.

> Innovation for women is innovation for everyone, and companies that understand that will own the future.

Equity as a Competitive Avantage

When companies commit to designing with women—meaningfully, consistently, and from the start—they create products that work better, last longer, and reach farther. Innovation for women is innovation for everyone, and companies that understand that will own the future.

Companies that design for equity outperform those that don't—not just socially or ethically, but financially, operationally, and strategically. These companies have:

- **Bigger, Real Markets:** Women are half the world. Emerging markets are most of the world. Building for them is the growth strategy.
- **Lower Failure Rates:** Products built for constrained environments become more resilient everywhere. Solutions built for convenience fall apart quickly.
- **Faster Adoption and Stickier Engagement:** Tools co-created with communities earn trust faster and stay embedded longer because they address actual needs, not imagined ones.
- **Policy and Procurement Alignment:** Governments, global funders, and major NGOs are increasingly prioritizing equity. Solutions that demonstrate real-world inclusion are more likely to be approved, reimbursed, procured, and scaled.

A PRACTICAL CHECKLIST FOR INNOVATORS

If you want your product to succeed in the real world—not just in a lab or investor pitch—pressure-test it with these questions:

- WHO WAS IN THE ROOM DESIGNING THIS? WHO WAS MISSING?
- DOES THIS WORK FOR THE WOMAN WITH THE FEWEST RESOURCES?
- WHAT ARE WE ASSUMING ABOUT LITERACY, PRIVACY, PHONE ACCESS, AGENCY, AND GENDER DYNAMICS?
- HOW COULD THIS PRODUCT PUT A WOMAN AT RISK?
- DOES IT REDUCE OR INCREASE WORKLOAD FOR FRONTLINE WORKERS?
- IS THE TOOL RESILIENT IN LOW-CONNECTIVITY, LOW-INFRASTRUCTURE ENVIRONMENTS?
- ARE WOMEN INVOLVED NOT JUST IN TESTING BUT IN DECISION-MAKING?
- IF THIS FAILS FOR THE MOST MARGINALIZED WOMAN, DO WE REDESIGN OR DO WE DISMISS HER AS AN "EDGE CASE"?

Your answers reveal whether you're building for impact or building for a press release.

- **Better Data and Better AI:** Tools designed for diverse populations produce richer, more accurate datasets. This strengthens clinical safety, AI performance, predictive accuracy, and long-term reliability. Companies building AI models on narrow datasets are building products that are already obsolete.
- **Stronger Brand Trust:** Women reward brands that show integrity and relevance. Trust becomes a strategic asset, especially in healthcare. Equity can't be a moral bonus; it's the high-performance strategy hiding in plain sight.

Raising the Standard

This chapter is ultimately about discipline: the discipline to rethink the default, rebuild what's outdated, and recognize that innovation can't be excellent if it excludes half the world. Innovation for women isn't niche. It's mainstream. It's profitable. It's required for companies that expect to compete in the next decade of healthcare and technology.

And the truth is: it's not hard to do. What's hard is pretending the old model still works.

The biggest misconception about innovating for women is that it requires a separate playbook. It doesn't. It requires discipline, representation, and a willingness to challenge the comfortable shortcuts that have shaped healthcare for decades. Companies don't need a "women's innovation strategy" layered on top of their existing work. They need an innovation strategy that's capable of serving half the human population without collapsing under its own biases.

When you strip this entire discussion down to its core, innovating for women is about raising the standard, not creating a different standard. It's about moving from "products that work for some people" to "products that work for the real world." And the real world is diverse: in bodies, behaviors, needs, environments, and experiences. Companies that embrace that reality move faster, fail less, and scale more sustainably.

The truth is, most companies aren't struggling because they lack technology or talent. They're struggling because their systems weren't built with enough perspectives to anticipate what's coming. Innovation slows down when every decision is filtered through the same set of lived experiences. It speeds up when the room expands.

Intentionality matters. If women aren't present in early product decision-making, they get relegated to "user testing" roles that surface problems far too late. Companies pay dearly for that. The cost of correcting baked-in bias after a product is built is exponentially higher than designing it correctly in the first place. That's why leading companies are shifting from "fix it downstream" to "design it upstream." It's efficient, it's strategic, and it's better business.

But companies can't simply increase representation and assume innovation will take care of itself. Representation must translate into influence. When women have real authority over R&D, product portfolio decisions, clinical strategy, regulatory direction, and investment priorities, there's a shift in how problems are defined and solved. The organization becomes more rigorous. The blind spots shrink. The work gets better.

The companies that are ahead today—across medtech, pharma, health tech, consumer health, AI, and diagnostics—share one thing in common: they built structures that force inclusion into the process. They redesigned their recruitment practices. They embedded equity reviews into product development. They required representative enrollment in trials. They funded women-led innovation internally. They engaged ERGs as strategic partners. They measured equity the same way they measured financial performance.

These operational decisions are returns on investment, returns on infrastructure building.

Companies that hesitate to include women find themselves increasingly out of step with the market and the workforce. Talented engineers, clinicians, and innovators won't stay in environments that refuse to evolve. Consumers won't buy from companies that ignore them. Regulators won't overlook blind spots that should have been redesigned years earlier. Investors won't tolerate outdated governance models.

The leaders who succeed will be the ones who understand that innovation is a perspective problem, not a pipeline problem. Fix the perspectives, and the pipeline follows.

This chapter isn't meant to be inspirational. It's meant to be direct: Innovating for women is the most effective, highest-return lever companies must pull to strengthen their products, their culture, their market position, and their future.

Not because women need special treatment. Not because it looks good on a DEI report. Not because it aligns with corporate values.

Innovating for women is the most effective, highest-return lever companies must pull to strengthen their products, their culture, their market position, and their future.

But because it produces superior innovation. Because it eliminates preventable failure. Because it builds organizations designed for the world as it is, not as it was. Because it's the only responsible way to build technology, devices, medicines, and systems meant for all humans.

Innovation for women is innovation for everyone.

Chapter 5 Takeaways

- **INNOVATION FAILS WHEN MEN ARE TREATED AS THE DEFAULT USER.** PRODUCTS, DEVICES, AND ALGORITHMS BUILT ON NARROW ASSUMPTIONS CREATE BLIND SPOTS, WEAKER PERFORMANCE, AND AVOIDABLE HARM.
- **DESIGNING FOR WOMEN IS HIGHER-STANDARD INNOVATION.** WHEN WOMEN SHAPE PRODUCTS UPSTREAM, COMPANIES BUILD BETTER SOLUTIONS, AVOID COSTLY REDESIGNS, AND SERVE REAL MARKETS MORE EFFECTIVELY.
- **EQUITY MUST BE BUILT INTO THE ARCHITECTURE, NOT ADDED LATER.** THE STRONGEST INNOVATIONS ARE DESIGNED FOR REAL-WORLD CONSTRAINTS: PRIVACY, LITERACY, SAFETY, INFRASTRUCTURE, AND CULTURAL CONTEXT.
- **COMPANIES THAT DESIGN FOR THE EDGES WILL OUTPERFORM THOSE THAT DESIGN FOR THE CENTER.** CO-CREATION, TRUST, AND INCLUSIVE DESIGN PRODUCE STRONGER PRODUCTS, FASTER ADOPTION, BETTER DATA, AND MORE DURABLE GROWTH.

Chapter 6: **Fund Differently**

If women's health is infrastructure, then the question is not only what we build but how we fund it. Many of the most promising innovations in women's health never fail scientifically. They fail financially. Capital flows toward known systems, and historically those systems weren't designed to support solutions built around women's needs across the full lifespan.

That's beginning to change. We'll start with the principles that allow innovations to scale without losing equity and examine case studies of reverse innovation emerging from resource-constrained environments. We'll end with a practical playbook for the investors and innovators deciding which ideas grow into lasting infrastructure and which remain stuck in pilot mode.

Design is where innovation begins; scale is where it fulfills its promise.

Scaling innovation in women's health means translating principles into practice across different contexts, cultures, and health systems. Copying a model and exporting it everywhere doesn't work.

The goal is adaptability. The strongest ideas are the ones that hold up under pressure, across geographies, and in systems that look nothing alike.

Because scale without equity isn't progress. It's repetition.

Redefining Scale

Scalable solutions are equitable solutions.

They're sustainable because they create lasting value for people, for systems, and for societies, not because they cost less. Scale is the discipline of durability. It's about designing impact that can withstand turnover, political change, and the expiration date on a grant.

For decades, the word "scale" has been used so casually in global health that it's lost meaning. Every proposal claims it, every conference celebrates it, and every report measures it in the easiest way possible: by counting outputs rather than outcomes—clinics built, women reached, vaccines delivered. But reach without permanence is noise, not progress.

In women's health, the problem is magnified. Projects expand quickly and collapse quietly. A maternal-health pilot launches with a splashy grant and vanishes once the press release fades. A new telehealth platform rolls out across five countries before anyone asks if women in rural areas even own smartphones. What we have scaled, over and over, is fragility disguised as success.

True scale regenerates. A scalable initiative is one that grows roots, not branches. It becomes part of the ecosystem rather than an imported species.

Jacaranda Health in Kenya is one of the clearest examples of a company that scaled by making existing infrastructure better, not by building more.

I first encountered Jacaranda in Nairobi during my time in the Senior Executive Program in Global Health Innovation Management with IESE Business School in 2019. I visited one of Jacaranda's clinics and watched the technology work in real time, with patients using a simple SMS-based platform to speak to their doctors. I've been following the company's evolution ever since.

After seeing women deliver their babies in facilities yet still die from preventable causes, Jacaranda's founder Nick Pearson realized quality of care was the issue, not access. The early model was a clinic. But one facility, no matter how well it runs, can't shift national outcomes. So Jacaranda pivoted from being a provider to creating PROMPTS, an AI-enabled digital health service that uses two-way SMS exchanges to empower women to seek care at the right time and place.

The platform runs on basic cellphones, not smartphones, because that's what the majority of users have. Short actionable messages, written for low-literacy contexts, go out in local languages. Shared-phone dynamics are accounted for, with sensitive content timed and phrased with safety in mind. It was co-created with midwives and frontline providers, ensuring that the tool supports their workflow instead of disrupting it.

Jacaranda became a partner with government systems and embedded quality improvement and digital feedback inside public facilities. It's what redefining scale looks like: Jacaranda built a digital layer that strengthens public health systems from within rather than replicating clinics. The company now reaches millions of mothers across Kenya, Ghana, and Eswatini, and has pilots running in several other East and West African countries through partnerships with thousands of public facilities. Maternal engagement rates sit at 60 to 70 percent or higher, strengthening national care quality at scale.

Scalability also means reengineering how we use existing assets. HERhealthEQ turns the waste stream of perfectly serviceable medical equipment that's been discarded because of replacement cycles into a supply chain by collecting, refurbishing, and redistributing it to hospitals and clinics in LMICs. It's the circular economy of care: closing loops instead of opening landfills.

This approach reframes the idea of aid entirely. Rather than sending cash or consumables, it transfers capability. Each delivery is technology and training, product and empowerment—the infrastructure to power what the local team needs and wants.

Sustainability in healthcare will not come from endless inventions but from intelligent reuse. The most scalable resources are the ones we already possess, redeployed where they are needed most.

The most durable examples of scale aren't coming from where most people expect. They're coming from the local areas where the innovations are serving needs.

Reverse Innovation

We are entering a decade defined by two simultaneous realities: a collapse in the legacy systems of HICs (those built for bureaucracy, not equity) and creation in emerging markets (new systems that are faster, cheaper, flexible, and more inclusive by design).

If the twentieth century's breakthroughs were medical, the twenty-first century's will be organizational. The next wave of innovation will not be imported from HICs to LMICs. They will be exported upward, from LMICs to the rest of the world. The future of women's health innovation is being built in Nairobi, Lagos, Bengaluru, Medellín, and beyond, not in San Francisco or Stockholm.

The old assumption that innovation flows from "advanced" economies to "developing" ones is collapsing under evidence. High-income countries are rich in resources but poor in flexibility. Their systems are bureaucratic, slow, and often paralyzed by regulation. In the US, it takes an average of seventeen years for a medical innovation to move from publication to routine clinical practice. That's not progress; it's stagnation with paperwork.

By contrast, low- and middle-income countries are unburdened by legacy systems. Lack of constraint has become their advantage. They can build healthcare architecture that fits today's technologies and tomorrow's markets instead of upgrading relics from the last century.

Reverse innovation—ideas traveling from south to north—is the new default.

Kenya's M-TIBA illustrates this inversion. I first heard about this program when I was spending time in Tanzania in 2017. I was learning about the healthcare system as HERhealthEQ's CEO while deploying medical equipment. I spent about seven weeks in East Africa, mainly in Tanzania, but traveled to Kenya twice. Mobile banking (called M-Pesa) was popularized in the 2010s beginning in Africa, well before high-income countries adopted the technology. The M-TIBA platform emerged from a partnership between CarePay, Safaricom, and PharmAccess to solve a core structural problem in African healthcare: people could not safely set aside or track money for health expenses, and providers lacked transparent payment systems. Built on Kenya's mobile money ecosystem, M-TIBA created a dedicated mobile health wallet that allows individuals, donors, insurers, and governments to send funds earmarked specifically for healthcare services at accredited facilities. It bypasses banks and insurers, placing financial control directly into women's hands. I thought it was brilliant, because when women have control of their finances, they have the ability to leverage it for healthcare.

The platform scaled rapidly by leveraging Safaricom's reach, integrating with thousands of clinics, and partnering with insurers and public programs. Millions of healthcare transactions later, M-TIBA

THE **THREE TESTS** OF SCALABILITY

When innovations are developed, their scale isn't limited to pilot projects, they should be designed to expand impact and distribution to reach the intended audience. To scale, they need to pass three "tests":

- **1. EQUITY.** DOES THE MODEL CLOSE GAPS OR WIDEN THEM? A TELEHEALTH PLATFORM THAT REQUIRES A HIGH-SPEED CONNECTION MAY REACH MILLIONS YET EXCLUDE THE VERY WOMEN WHO NEED IT MOST. SCALE WITHOUT EQUITY IS EXPANSION OF BIAS.
- **2. SUSTAINABILITY.** DOES IT SURVIVE THE END OF FUNDING? A CLINIC THAT CLOSES WHEN A GRANT ENDS WAS NEVER SCALABLE; IT WAS SUBSIDIZED. REAL SUSTAINABILITY COMES WHEN INCENTIVES FOR EVERY STAKEHOLDER ALIGN AND THE WORK CONTINUES.
- **3. OWNERSHIP.** DO THE PEOPLE SERVED WANT TO SUSTAIN IT? PROGRAMS IMPOSED FROM THE OUTSIDE UNRAVEL WHEN SUPPORT IS WITHDRAWN. THOSE BUILT WITH LOCAL PARTICIPATION PERSIST BECAUSE COMMUNITIES CHOOSE TO KEEP THEM ALIVE.

When these three tests are met simultaneously, growth becomes self-propelling.

has expanded financial protection for low-income households and improved data transparency for funders and policymakers, turning fragmented out-of-pocket spending into trackable, targeted health financing infrastructure.

While the US debates interoperability standards, Nairobi's innovators have already operationalized them. LMICs are laboratories for the future of healthcare. The challenge for HICs is humility: to recognize that "less" infrastructure can mean more adaptability. In LMICs, scarcity is a forcing function: it demands solutions that are practical, low-cost, and scalable by necessity.

Innovation no longer trickles down; it radiates outward.

Take Butterfly Network for example, a company I have worked with through HERhealthEQ to deploy its technology. It was founded by physician-entrepreneur Jonathan Rothberg after witnessing the limitations of bulky, $50,000+ ultrasound machines that left frontline clinicians without imaging when they needed it most. The idea was radical but simple: put ultrasound on a silicon chip and connect it to a smartphone.

Innovation no longer trickles down; it radiates outward.

That breakthrough produced Butterfly iQ, a handheld, whole-body imaging device priced at a fraction of the cost of traditional systems. The company scaled through regulatory approvals in dozens of countries, hospital partnerships, global health deployments, and education platforms that trained non-radiologists in point-of-care imaging. Today, Butterfly devices are used in more than one hundred countries, including rural India, Nigeria, and Mexico, where midwives and nurses now perform prenatal scans in community clinics instead of referring women to distant hospitals. HERhealthEQ has deployed more than thirty Butterfly iQ systems and has plans for continued growth, as it puts healthcare at the point-of-care.

Butterfly Network is expanding access to obstetric care, emergency diagnostics, and primary care imaging, especially in low-resource settings, while fundamentally redefining imaging as portable infrastructure rather than fixed capital equipment. It's cheaper, faster, safer, and more empowering than using bulky ultrasound machines.

The principle of constraint-driven innovation that produced portable ultrasounds also produced a new model for blood supply logistics. Constraint-driven innovation is the true "direct to consumer" model for healthcare, when it's not only focused on apps and tracking health but delivering care to the resource constrained patients where it's needed directly.

During her pregnancy, Temie Giwa-Tubosun experienced a severe hemorrhage. Thankfully, she was in the US and received the immediate care and blood transfusions she needed, so she and the baby are OK. But this experience made her realize that in her home country of Nigeria, where blood shortages are common, the same complication is often fatal.

She built LifeBank in Nigeria to solve the blood supply crisis through a pay-per-use logistics model. Using cold-chain tech, mapping software, and a mobile platform, LifeBank now connects hospitals to verified blood banks and delivers blood, oxygen, and vaccines to hospitals on demand through data-driven distribution networks.

> These innovations emerged not despite scarcity but because of it.

Scaling through partnerships with state governments, private hospitals, and international funders, LifeBank expanded across multiple Nigerian states and into Kenya and Ethiopia, integrating digital inventory management and demand forecasting to reduce waste. The company saves thousands of lives every year, has dramatically reduced blood stock-outs in partner facilities, and can respond quickly to obstetric emergencies—directly addressing one of the leading causes of maternal mortality in the region. And it's profitable.

These innovations emerged not despite scarcity but because of it.

High-income systems are optimized for compliance, not creativity. They measure success in process adherence and risk avoidance. That culture produces safety but not speed. Facing urgent need, LMIC innovators reverse the equation. They design for speed and iterate toward safety.

Consider how quickly Southeast Asia and Africa adopted mobile banking compared to the West. Mobile banking launched in the Philippines in the early 2000s and then rapidly scaled the fastest throughout Kenya, where it launched in 2007. Within three years, Kenya's mobile banking M-Pesa had more than 9 million users, who hadn't previously had access to banking services. Within five years, M-Pesa reached two-thirds of Kenyan adults. Today, 90 percent of all Kenyan adults use it, and more than 60 percent of adults in countries such as Bangladesh, Uganda, Ghana, and Tanzania use it.

Healthcare follows the same trajectory. The continent's digital-first infrastructure allows payment, records, and teleconsultation to converge seamlessly. Where Europe struggles with data privacy bureaucracy, Rwanda has already implemented national digital health IDs.

The lesson is simple: scalability favors flexibility. A system too rigid to adapt can't grow. The very complexity that made HIC healthcare impressive in the twentieth century makes it unsustainable in the twenty-first.

The next era of scalable innovation will come from middle-income countries (MICs)—India, Brazil, Kenya, Indonesia, Mexico—where healthcare spending is growing faster than GDP. According to IMF projections, 1.5 billion people will join the middle class by 2030. Their first discretionary purchase is healthcare.

The US market is saturated and margins are shrinking. Meanwhile, MICs are growing markets that can absorb and adapt to new technologies faster. They've moved past "developing" and are now defining. These countries are proving that inclusion is an act of competitive advantage. Companies that ignore these markets will miss the future of growth.

Financing Innovation and Building Durable Models

Scale begins with design but lives or dies with financing. Because innovation without financing is a prototype; financing without innovation is bureaucracy. The two together create transformation.

Innovation fails because good ideas run out of funding that fits them. Too many promising programs reach a plateau because the money is wrong, not the model. The dominant financing architecture in global health is designed for projects, not systems. It rewards novelty, not continuity.

Short-term grants fund pilots that can never mature. Governments and foundations push for immediate, reportable impact. But the problems we're trying to solve—maternal mortality, access inequities, chronic disease—require decades of consistent investment. Scale can't be achieved with one-year money for twenty-year problems.

Women's health needs capital that behaves differently: long-term, flexible, risk-tolerant, and aligned with public good and private sustainability. That kind of money doesn't just fund programs; it builds infrastructure.

BLENDED FINANCE: REENGINEERING RISK

Blended finance is the foundation of the next wave of scalable impact. It combines concessional capital (from governments or philanthropies) with private investment to share risk and attract scale. Instead of waiting for markets to "mature," blended finance matures them.

The Global Innovation Fund (GIF) demonstrates this model clearly. It funds solutions that deliver measurable social returns while also showing potential for market sustainability. Each tranche of financing (grants, loans, and equity) is structured to match the venture's level of maturity. The risk of early failure is borne by donors, and the rewards of success attract investors. For every public dollar, GIF mobilizes roughly four from private capital. That's scale by design, not by accident.

Blended finance flips the old model of dependency on its head. It creates confidence. It tells investors: "You won't be alone." And confidence, not capital, is often what drives expansion.

CATALYTIC PHILANTHROPY: THE BRIDGE BETWEEN VISION AND MARKET

Traditional philanthropy gives, while catalytic philanthropy multiplies. It treats money as a tool for leverage, not ownership.

Melinda French Gates's Pivotal has become a blueprint for this approach. Pivotal invests across the continuum of gender equity: healthcare, workforce participation, and technology access. Its funding is infrastructure. By seeding funds, influencing policy, investing in innovations, and mobilizing networks, it changes the conditions in which innovation happens.

Catalytic philanthropy is risk-tolerant capital. It steps in early, funds policy change, and attracts commercial partners later. Instead of solving one problem, it redefines the market so that the next generation of innovators can solve a hundred more.

This approach is how we stop treating women's health as an underfunded niche and start treating it as a growth sector.

VENTURE PHILANTHROPY: PROFIT AS A PATH TO PERMANENCE

Venture philanthropy takes this one step further. It combines the rigor of venture investing with the mission of philanthropy. The goal is to generate permanent returns, not outsized ones.

Jacaranda Health in Kenya, which I mentioned earlier as a model of scale, also illustrates what venture philanthropy can achieve. The company has been backed by venture philanthropy and impact-first capital, including Acumen and the Global Innovation Fund. The early phase was funded by philanthropic capital to prove the concept. Once validated, Jacaranda transitioned to a hybrid model: revenue from government contracts, licensing of its digital tools, and partnerships with local hospitals.

That shift turned a donor-dependent program into a business-like enterprise embedded in the national healthcare system. It can now grow on the strength of its results, not the generosity of its donors.

Venture philanthropy treats sustainability as the real ROI. When a philanthropic dollar creates a system that can fund itself, that's the highest possible return.

Scalable systems need new structures, not just new funding. The sharp distinction between "for-profit" and "nonprofit" is an artifact of the twentieth century. The most effective models of the twenty-first century blur the line entirely.

REVENUE-GENERATING NONPROFITS

Organizations like Living Goods embody this evolution. Operating in Uganda and Kenya, Living Goods trains women as community health entrepreneurs, giving them tablets, diagnostic tools, and affordable medicines to sell. These women earn commissions, which sustains their engagement. Communities get access to low-cost care, and the organization achieves revenue flow that reduces reliance on external grants.

The model works because it builds a workforce that benefits personally from systemic success. When doing good is also good business, you don't have to force participation. It sustains itself, and it has measurable outcomes, such as a 27 percent reduction in under-five child mortality, especially through the distribution of appropriate treatments for malaria, diarrhea, pneumonia, and family planning needs. Living Good has more than 12,000 community health workers supporting 8 to 10 million people annually with an estimated cost of roughly $68 per life saved.

It's a textbook example of aligned incentives. When women make a living by improving health outcomes, every sale is both an economic and social transaction. Scale becomes inevitable because motivation becomes intrinsic.

FOR-PROFITS WITH PURPOSE

Then there are companies like mPharma in Ghana, which redesigned the pharmaceutical supply chain across Africa. By pooling purchasing power and centralizing inventory, mPharma cut retail drug prices by up to 60 percent while maintaining profitability. Its platform gives independent pharmacies real-time data and financing options, allowing them to thrive rather than fold.

mPharma's impact is structural. It made drugs cheaper and the system smarter. That's what scalability looks like when business models are aligned with social needs. It's corporate self-interest redefined: purpose is the reason business exists.

BLENDED ECOSYSTEMS

Sometimes scalability emerges from integration, not invention. India's Narayana Health demonstrates how. I first learned about the network while in IESE Business School, and the scale, the system of efficiency, and the blended model intrigued me, as it creates a system of opportunity for all patients without solely a charitable focus. Founded by cardiac surgeon Dr. Devi Shetty, the hospital network transformed access to heart surgery by combining public insurance programs, private pay patients, philanthropy, and high-volume clinical care within a single system.

Patients who can afford care pay market rates, while low-income patients receive treatment through government insurance or charitable support. State health programs subsidize procedures for poorer patients, nonprofit partners help connect rural populations to care, and private revenue helps fund expansion and technological investment. The ecosystem is deliberately blended: each stakeholder contributes a different part of the financing and delivery structure. It creates the infrastructure that helps societies scale healthcare and their communities locally.

The results are remarkable. Narayana Health performs tens of thousands of cardiac surgeries each year, often at a fraction of the cost of comparable procedures in high-income countries, while maintaining clinical outcomes comparable to leading hospitals worldwide. It scaled not only through surgical efficiency, but by designing a system that works across public programs, private finance, and community access. That's the future of scalability: systems built on collaboration rather than isolation.

Investment Landscape

Over a twenty-five year window, women's health produced more than 276 exits, more than $100 billion in deal value, and twenty-seven billion-dollar deals. The 2026 *Follow the Exits* report from AOA Dx is the first to count them correctly. What the market called oncology exits were breast cancer exits. What it called general medtech was women's health medtech. The category existed. The accounting didn't.

The momentum has been accelerating in the last five years. The most active women's health company in the data is my former employer, Hologic. Two of the top seven exits were deals I worked on directly. I'm sharing this because the people building the market have known what it was for decades. The numbers are finally catching up.

When the data gets mapped to reality instead of legacy categories, the investment case stops being a pitch. It becomes math.

The transition from aid to investment thinking marks a paradigm shift. Donors and investors alike are recognizing that social impact and financial return are no longer at odds. Impact investing and gender-lens funds now target ventures that improve health outcomes while generating measurable returns.

Women's health funds have multiplied and are deploying real capital. Angel investors—largely women who invest because they have lived the gaps themselves—are stepping in earlier and more aggressively. Corporate venture arms are building women's health strategies across pharma, medtech, imaging, and even consumer health because it expands their revenue base. Member associations like the American Heart Association are creating venture vehicles to invest in the innovations their membership needs.

Philanthropy remains vital, but its role is changing. Instead of funding perpetual dependency, large philanthropic players are providing unrestricted, catalytic capital that de-risks early development. Government-backed initiatives are creating new reimbursement and procurement pathways. International development agencies are funding maternal, cancer, and chronic health innovation. Emerging markets like Africa, Latin America, and India are creating their own investment ecosystems focused on local women's health innovation. It's an ecosystem forming in real time.

This is where alternative funding models become a strategic advantage, not an afterthought. Women's health companies often thrive with blended capital.

For example:

- Women's health funds can supply early lead capital.
- Angel syndicates provide fast checks and deep community amplification.
- Corporate venture offers distribution and data.
- Philanthropic capital funds early validation.
- Associations (e.g., cardiovascular, oncology, maternal health) create venture vehicles to fund mission-aligned innovation.

A NEW ECONOMIC MANDATE: **MEASURE THE RIGHT THINGS**

The world has been optimizing for the wrong metrics. GDP ignores unpaid care. Corporate dashboards ignore long-term productivity. Health systems ignore quality of life and preventive savings. Investment frameworks ignore intergenerational impact.

To correct this, leaders must adopt a new set of measures:

- **HEALTH-ADJUSTED WORKFORCE PARTICIPATION:** TRACKING WHO IS HEALTHY ENOUGH TO WORK AND THRIVE, INSTEAD OF JUST WHO IS WORKING.
- **CARE ECONOMY CONTRIBUTION:** VALUING UNPAID CARE AS THE ECONOMIC ENGINE IT IS.
- **INTERGENERATIONAL HUMAN CAPITAL IMPACT:** MODELING FUTURE GDP ON CHILDREN'S OUTCOMES TIED TO MATERNAL HEALTH, NOT JUST ON CURRENT LABOR.
- **MIDLIFE RETENTION INDEX:** TRACKING HOW WELL WORKPLACES SUPPORT WOMEN AT THE HEIGHT OF THEIR EXPERIENCE.
- **PREVENTIVE CARE ROI:** QUANTIFYING LONG-TERM SAVINGS FROM SHORT-TERM HEALTH INVESTMENTS.

When you measure the right things, you fund the right things.

The result is systems that grow stronger, smarter, and more sustainable. Systems that expand opportunity rather than shrink it. Systems that reflect the full workforce they rely on.

- Emerging market funds invest in models Western VCs overlook.
- Revenue-generating nonprofit arms create stable income that supports research and development.
- Generalist funds allocating a percentage to women's health increase downstream investment.

This layered capital approach strengthens the company's position. Dependence on a single capital type equals fragility. Diversification equals durability.

And in that environment, investors need to hear a message many innovators hesitate to say plainly: women's health is one of the highest-return opportunities in global healthcare.

The market fundamentals are strong. The gaps are massive. The consumer demand is unavoidable. And the first companies that build trust, distribution, and clinical credibility will dominate categories that have been stagnant for decades.

Women's health is one of the highest-return opportunities in global healthcare.

Both Sides of the Table

I pitched DeepLook Medical to an angel investor group seven times. I answered every question clearly and thoroughly, spending more than twelve hours with the group in addition to sending what felt like every single document the company had created.

After seven meetings with no commitment, I brought my white, bald, male CFO into the eighth meeting. I gave him scripted answers to the questions I knew they'd ask—the same answers I'd given multiple times myself. He read them, and the investors committed their capital. I knew exactly why: the answers hadn't changed, but the person delivering them had. It made my blood boil. But I knew that if I wanted that capital for my company, I had to play the game. So I played it. It's an experiment I conducted, wishing I wasn't correct in my assumptions but proving that I was.

I've sat on both sides of this table. I've invested in women's health companies and funds. I've also stood in front of investor groups pitching my own companies, answering questions about a space most of the people in the room knew nothing about. This dual perspective is why I'm not going to tell innovators how to pitch or tell investors how to evaluate. I'm going to describe what the table looks like when this conversation goes well, so that both sides recognize what they need to bring.

These insights come directly from my experiences and from many of my colleagues throughout the years. They are not hypothetical learnings or examples.

WHAT INVESTORS NEED TO UNDERSTAND

I'm an investor in Portfolia, one of the largest women's health combined funds that has since raised two additional women's health specific funds and more than a dozen women-focused funds. The portfolio of companies span women's health and consumer goods for women. Several are already showing returns, and many are working toward exits. My investment wasn't large. It was a way for me to explore investing in funds and gain an understanding of how the system works from the inside. I've participated in deal meetings, reviewed draft deal memos, watched due diligence happen in real time, and learned the mechanics of how capital flows into companies. This helped to inform my work as I joined investment committees for women's health funds globally. It taught me what investors are looking for when they sit down at this table:

The market is mispriced, not unproven. Despite the ROI I laid out in Chapter 4, women's health remains underfunded. Not because it lacks potential, but because it has been chronically misclassified as niche, as emotional, as "impact," as something outside the commercial core of healthcare. That misclassification is the opportunity. It's a mispriced market, and mispriced markets are exactly where early investors make their strongest returns.

Unfamiliarity is not a risk. Most investors are men. Most of them have never experienced the problems firsthand, and many haven't studied sex-based physiology, regulatory nuance, or global market differences. That lack of familiarity feels like risk. But risk is often just information they don't yet have. And it's precisely where early-stage investors have historically made their best returns.

The market rewards patience and precision. Women's health companies often scale better when they grow in stages: direct-to-consumer revenue first, then payer contracts, then platform expansion. Regulatory paths and clinical validation take time. Reimbursements may be a future lever, not an immediate one.

WHAT INNOVATORS NEED TO BRING TO THE TABLE

Commercial clarity. Investors want specifics: the exact population, the exact problem, the commercial path, the regulatory path, and the exit scenario. Women's health is dozens of categories: oncology, cardiovascular disease, menopause, fertility, maternal health, autoimmune disease, sexual health, workplace health, digital therapeutics, chronic disease, diagnostics, imaging, global health delivery, and AI trained on female physiology. Investors know how to price clear categories. They don't know how to price vague missions.

I'm also an investor in Ultrasound AI, a maternal health predictive AI company I consulted for and advised. The founder started from a personal experience and a dream, built the algorithm, conducted proof-of-concept work outside the US, and received US Food and Drug Administration approval. The personal story got people's attention. The commercial strategy and the market size got their money.

Precision on the known friction points. What investors appreciate even more are innovators who address known friction points upfront. Women's health has several: clinical skepticism due to decades of male-default research; stigma around sexual, reproductive, and hormonal health; patchy reimbursement; fragmented care pathways; inconsistent global infrastructure; and regulatory and marketing barriers. Investors want to know the plan to navigate these with operational strategy, not idealism.

Discipline on scope. Women's health companies typically don't have a single product. But the companies that will lead are those that start with a wedge and expand into a broader ecosystem—menopause plus cardiovascular risk, fertility plus chronic disease management, HPV testing plus cervical cancer pathways. Investors respond to companies who articulate, "Here's our wedge, here's the near-term total addressable market, here's why we win here first." A focused early approach prevents dilution of effort and capital.

WHAT BOTH SIDES NEED FROM EACH OTHER.

Alignment matters more than capital. This is especially true in women's health, where companies face stigma, nuance, regulatory complexity, and cultural sensitivity. Innovators should be evaluating investors just as rigorously as they're being evaluated. What's your thesis in women's health? How do you support companies navigating clinical or regulatory processes? How many women-led companies have you funded? How do you evaluate success in categories with stigma? Do you reserve follow-on capital? What part of the market are you most bullish on? Their answers reveal everything.

The best pitches feel like an inevitability, not persuasion. Women's health isn't a temporary boom. It's a sustained trend fueled by demographics, economics, clinical evidence, workforce dynamics, and cultural transformation. Innovations that solve real, burning, daily problems are being created. Global markets are growing faster than most US-based investors understand. That combination—real need, cultural momentum, and demographic inevitability—is what makes women's health such a powerful investment opportunity. When all of this is articulated with clarity, the pitch shifts from persuasion to inevitability.

Why am I telling you this from personal experience, not just observation? The table is almost never fair, and you must decide how you're going to navigate that.

Several years ago, I pitched at an invited angel investor event. Investors chose to attend, so I assumed they were interested in the industry. About seven minutes into my presentation, a gentleman in his seventies unmuted himself, interrupted me, and asked, "Is breast cancer really still a thing?" He didn't ask if breast cancer was still a problem... he asked if it was still a "thing". Sadly, I've encountered men like this many times before. I stared into the camera, calmly responded "yes," and kept going.

I finished the pitch, and I answered questions from people who clearly knew nothing about this area of health. Afterward, I emailed the group coordinator and respectfully declined to pursue the opportunity with the group. I wasn't in a position to turn down money. My company was running on fumes, but I knew I couldn't take money from a group who had people like that. When we, as women, look for investment, we must stay true to our values, while adapting to ensure the longevity of our companies.

That's why we need more women investing, more women at the table, and more women in positions where they can change the dynamics of these rooms from the inside. But they're not the whole picture, and I don't want to leave the impression that this market is defined by its friction. The friction is real, and it needs to be named. But the momentum is also real, and it's accelerating. The companies being built today will shape healthcare for the next fifty years.

Durability

Scalable systems produce what economists call the durability dividend: the long-term savings and stability that come when health becomes predictable. Preventing a maternal death saves far more than it costs. It stabilizes the workforce, protects education outcomes, and strengthens GDP.

In countries that have invested in women's health systematically, the effects are visible at every level:

- Lower fertility rates correlate with higher female labor-force participation.
- Fewer maternal deaths mean fewer orphans, reducing social welfare costs.
- Healthier women start more businesses, invest more in their families, and pay more taxes.

Durability is fiscal responsibility. It's the compound interest of good policy.

The global health community talks about sustainability, but what it really means is predictability—systems that can plan, budget, and adapt year after year without external rescue. That's what scalability must achieve: dependable permanence, not endless growth.

Zipline perfectly illustrates scaling to permanence.

PITCH **PERFECT**

Investors look for innovators who understand risk. They want to know how you'll de-risk your science, your regulatory plan, your go-to-market strategy, and your distribution. They want to see partnerships that validate your model. They want early signals: pilots, clinical advisors, health system interest, employer letters of intent, international demand, or IP that creates genuine defensibility. They want to know that you know how to navigate friction points that are predictable in women's health: political scrutiny, cultural sensitivity, regulatory lag, and stigma.

And they want to know you can communicate complexity cleanly. Women's health is clinically dense, socially layered, and structurally outdated. You need to translate that without turning your pitch into a lecture. Investors want innovators who can articulate: "Here's the problem. Here's the cost. Here's the solution. Here's why we win."

The bar for women pitching in this space is higher than it should be. That's the reality. Women must quantify and justify the market, the clinical path, the commercial logic, and the exit scenario with more precision than male counterparts. To all the women who are doing the hard work: do it anyway, until the room changes.

Several truths matter here:

- **"NO COMPETITORS" IS A RED FLAG.** THERE ARE ALWAYS COMPETITORS: HEALTH SYSTEMS, EXISTING PROTOCOLS, OUTDATED DEVICES, UNREGULATED SUPPLEMENTS, LEGACY INCUMBENTS, OR CUSTOMER BEHAVIOR ITSELF. BUT SINCE WOMEN'S HEALTH IS A "NEW" MARKET THAT HASN'T HAD INNOVATION OR DISRUPTION, THERE ALSO MIGHT NOT BE TRUE COMPETITORS.

- **KNOW YOUR ECONOMICS.** BE CLEAR. WOMEN'S HEALTH CARRIES QUANTIFIABLE COSTS. SHOW HOW YOUR UNIT ECONOMICS CAN SCALE IN HIGH- AND MIDDLE-INCOME SETTINGS.
- **A PERSONAL STORY CAN HELP OR HURT.** USE IT ONLY IF IT STRENGTHENS, NOT REPLACES, THE COMMERCIAL LOGIC. UNDERSTAND YOUR AUDIENCE AND WHEN TO USE YOUR STORY.
- **INVESTORS DON'T FUND POTENTIAL; THEY FUND READINESS.** REGULATORY CLARITY, DISTRIBUTION STRATEGY, TEAM STRENGTH, AND CLINICAL RIGOR SIGNAL READINESS. SHOW THAT YOU ARE SOLVING A CLINICAL PROBLEM IN ADDITION TO A CONVENIENCE PROBLEM.
- **POLITICAL VOLATILITY IS A LIABILITY.** SHOW HOW YOUR MODEL IS NOT VULNERABLE TO POLICY SWINGS, MARKETING LIMITATIONS, OR IDEOLOGICAL NOISE.
- **KNOW YOUR PATH TO LIQUIDITY.** ARTICULATE YOUR EXIT PLANS, YOUR GROWTH TARGETS, AND HOW YOU WILL ACHIEVE THEM. KNOW THE MARKET, THE COMPARABLES, AND THE CYCLES.
- **YOU ARE ALSO EVALUATING THEM.** IF AN INVESTOR WANTS YOU TO PIVOT INTO SOMETHING IRRELEVANT JUST TO MATCH THEIR THESIS, WALK AWAY. MISALIGNED CAPITAL IS EXPENSIVE CAPITAL.

I found Zipline on a crowdfunding site in 2016 when they were just starting to grow on a small scale. A robotics company using autonomous drones to deliver blood and medical supplies to rural health facilities in Africa was an unheard-of idea at the time. I invested because I understood the problem they were solving.

Patients in Rwanda were dying from stockouts of blood and critical medicines because there was no reliable way to get them from a central supply to a rural clinic in time. But instead of piloting small NGO programs, Zipline partnered directly with national governments (Rwanda first, then Ghana), integrating into public supply chains and proving reliability at national scale.

Zipline now completes hundreds of thousands of autonomous deliveries in Rwanda and Ghana, serving thousands of health facilities and dramatically reducing blood, vaccine, and emergency medicine stockouts nationwide. These deliveries have resulted in a 56 percent decrease in maternal mortality, 66 percent decrease in missed opportunities to treat malaria, and 60 percent shorter stockouts.

Zipline scaled not because of its drones but because of its design. Its service fits seamlessly into health systems rather than sitting on top of them. That's the future of scalability: interdependence without inefficiency.

The True Measure of Success

For most modern global health, success has meant scale in numbers—how many lives touched, how many clinics built, how many units distributed. But numbers can lie. They count activity, not resilience.

Real success looks different:

- When a program survives leadership turnover without collapse
- When a clinic continues operating after a donor exits
- When a model is copied without needing a manual

Programs like HERhealthEQ, Jacaranda Health, Butterfly Network, Lifebank, and Zipline embody this form of success. Each has proven that scalability isn't about inventing new things; it's about creating conditions where solutions sustain themselves.

HERhealthEQ's equipment keeps functioning because hospitals are trained to maintain it. Jacaranda's maternal-health platform keeps expanding because it's embedded in government contracts. Butterfly's handheld ultrasound grows because it aligns with existing clinical workflows. Lifebank thrives because it monetized logistics instead of depending on subsidies. Zipline gained permanence through government partnerships and expanding distribution.

They've all built systems that want to survive.

That's the metric global health should adopt next: desire to persist. When a system's users and operators are motivated to maintain it, it can endure anything—political upheaval, funding gaps, even global crises.

The next decade will separate systems that talk about scale from those that achieve it. The difference will be governance, not gadgets.

High-income countries will need to unlearn complexity; low- and middle-income countries will need to leverage flexibility. The path forward will depend on three principles:

1. **Equity as efficiency.** When everyone participates, systems function better. Fairness is a design feature, not an add-on.
1. **Finance as fuel, not control.** Sustainable capital empowers momentum.
1. **Leadership transfer.** True scalability happens when those who start systems prepare to step aside.

This is the quiet revolution of our time: shifting from charity to capacity, from programs to permanence, from innovation as experiment to innovation as infrastructure. Scaling women's health is about lasting for generations, not just about reaching millions. Because the real measure of innovation is not how fast it spreads, but how long it lasts.

Innovation and scale that last do so because of the real partnerships between the companies, women, communities, institutions, and capital sources.

Chapter 6 Takeaways

- **REAL SCALE IS ACHIEVED THROUGH MULTIPLE TYPES OF FUNDING, NOT ONE ALONE.** SOLUTIONS ONLY SCALE WHEN THEY ARE DURABLE, EQUITABLE, LOCALLY OWNED, AND BUILT TO SURVIVE BEYOND GRANTS, FOUNDERS, AND POLITICAL CYCLES.
- **INVESTMENT ALIGNMENT IS CRITICAL TO ACHIEVE SHARED GOALS.** ALL SIDES OF CAPITAL ALLOCATION MUST HAVE ALIGNMENT FOR THE SUCCESS AND PROSPERITY OF ALL SOLUTIONS, INSTEAD OF ONE-SIDED WIN-LOSE ECONOMICS.
- **THE FUTURE OF SCALABLE INNOVATION IS COMING FROM EMERGING MARKETS AND BLENDED MODELS.** LMICS ARE PROVING THAT FLEXIBLE, CONSTRAINT-DRIVEN SYSTEMS CAN OUTPERFORM LEGACY MODELS IN SPEED, ACCESS, AND ADAPTABILITY.
- **WOMEN'S HEALTH IS A MISPRICED MARKET AND ONE OF THE HIGHEST-RETURN OPPORTUNITIES IN HEALTHCARE.** THE WINNERS WILL BE THE INVESTORS AND OPERATORS WHO TREAT WOMEN'S HEALTH AS A LONG-TERM GROWTH SECTOR, NOT A NICHE CATEGORY.

Chapter 7: **Partner Differently**

Partnership is one of the most overused words in global health, and yet one of the least practiced with integrity. Everyone claims they "partner" with communities, institutions, and women. But partnership isn't a slogan. It's not a donor logo on a banner or a handshake photo taken after a deal was already negotiated in a conference room far from the people who will live with the consequences. Real partnership demands humility, shared power, and a willingness to recognize that the best ideas rarely come from the top floor of a building in Geneva, Washington, London, or New York. They come from people, mostly women, who are solving problems every day with almost no resources and zero recognition.

The world has a long track record of calling something a partnership when what it truly is, is paternalism dressed up with nicer language. Donors dictate solutions, governments sign off for the sake of funding, and communities are expected to adapt to innovations designed without them. Then we act surprised when those solutions fail. If we want lasting progress in women's health, we need to retire these outdated, top-down models. Women don't need to be "saved." They need to be taken seriously.

The truth is simple: nothing about women's global health works unless women are seated at the table, have real influence, and are treated as co-architects of the solutions intended for them. That includes women across geographies, backgrounds, income levels, religions, and lived experiences. It includes men too—not as spokespersons for women, but as allies who carry weight in systems still wired to respond more quickly when a man speaks. Diversity of thought is not a nice-to-have. It's the only path to designing solutions that match the complexity of health systems and the realities of the billions of women they're meant to serve.

I had to learn much of this the hard way—failed projects, lived innovation pipelines not optimized for my needs, and living in different countries and cultures to understand how to best partner globally. And trust me, I'm not perfect at it.

Listening is a strategy. Solutions fall apart because the people closest to the problem weren't asked how they solve it today, what stands in their way, or what would make a difference tomorrow. Instead, they're expected to "receive" innovation. That's not partnership.

You can't "partner" while hoarding information. You can't "partner" while designing solutions in closed rooms. And you can't "partner" while treating women, communities, or local organizations as passive implementation arms. Real partnership distributes power. Real partnership gives credit where it's due. Real partnership is uncomfortable, because it forces institutions to accept that they don't always know best, even when they have the most money.

Partnership requires a shift in mindset long before a contract is signed or a pilot is launched. It asks us to interrogate the assumptions we've been trained to carry into global health: that solutions need to be "scaled" through Western institutions to be legitimate, that anything created in a low- or middle-income country must be "strengthened" by international expertise, that women's insights are secondary to the insights of subject-matter experts who often have never lived the reality they're trying to solve. These assumptions are subtle, but they show up everywhere: in funding proposals, product roadmaps, clinical protocols, and the way we talk about global women's health.

> Partnership means distributing leadership to the right people at the right moments, without diluting accountability.

The irony is that when partnerships function correctly, everything becomes easier. Decision-making is faster. Adoption is seamless. Community trust grows instead of eroding. And women become the driving force behind scale.

Partnership doesn't mean endless consensus-building until no one wants the product anymore. It means distributing leadership to the right people at the right moments, without diluting accountability. It means acknowledging that knowledge is contextual, and those closest to the problem should shape the solution, even if institutional instinct tells us we know better.

Systems Are People

Most people look at institutions—the WHO, the FDA, a congressional committee, an insurance company's coverage board—and see walls. That's because from the outside, institutions look fortified: committees, hierarchies, acronyms, protocols, and decades of "how things have always been done." They see bureaucracy and decide the effort isn't worth it.

I used to think that too. But institutions aren't monoliths. They're collections of individuals that can be reached. The policy staffer who's been waiting for better data. The legislator who cares but hasn't heard from a constituent who can explain the problem in plain language. The committee member who needs one credible voice to justify the vote they want to cast. I learned this by showing up, telling my story, and discovering that the people on the other side of the table were allies who hadn't been activated yet.

As I mentioned in my personal breast imaging story (in Chapter 3), I'm among the 50 percent of women globally that have dense breast tissue.

In 2023, the FDA published a rule that requires mammography reports to include dense breast notification, and it went into effect in September 2024. But being notified without insurance covering additional imaging is like getting a cancer diagnosis without a treatment plan. The next step is to ensure that all women, federally, have insurance coverage for the additional imaging that's needed to clearly visualize their breast tissue.

When I became the CEO of DeepLook Medical, the loudest legislative leader speaking about dense breast legislation was Representative Rosa DeLauro of Connecticut. At that time, the company was based in her district, so it was natural to connect with her and tell her team about the work we do. That connection introduced me to leaders in advocacy and I started to learn about how regular people, like myself, could use our voices to make legislative change. After being exposed to the space and the leaders who focused on breast cancer early detection, I joined the bi-partisan advocacy group Breast Cancer Early Detection Coalition (BCEDC) as a steering committee member.

In September 2024, the larger team came together to lobby in the halls of Congress and the House of Representatives in Washington DC. We met with more than fifteen legislators including then-senate majority leader Charles Schumer (D-NY) and Debbie Wasserman-Shultz (D-FL), who is a breast cancer survivor, alongside their health leaders to explain the problem and why national dense breast insurance coverage for additional imaging is needed.

In every conversation, there was a representative from a breast company, someone who had dense breasts, and many who had previously battled breast cancer and survived. After almost every discussion was a head nod or a personal story from the staffer, the health leader, or the legislative leader themselves. They understood it because it was personal and it made sense. A year later we secured bi-partisan co-sponsors of the bill at both the House and Congressional levels. It took many meetings, many advocacy days, many phone calls, and encouraging everyone we knew to write letters.

Currently, insurance coverage for additional imaging is decided at the state level, which is inherently inequitable. Federal coverage would mean women across the country have the ability to access the correct imaging for their body. This is most impactful because when the US makes changes like this, global health leadership often follows.

This work continues. As I write this, half of all US states have coverage. There's also a bill on the floor for vote, with strong support thanks to our collective work, that is hopeful to pass in 2026.

Systems weren't designed to be immutable. They're human-made and human-changeable.

Systems weren't designed to be immutable. They're human-made and human-changeable. The inequities that define women's healthcare are design flaws, and those can be corrected.

Every generation has the opportunity to rebuild what it inherits. Dr. Bernadine Healy's editorial that I mentioned in Chapter 2 exposed the consequences of omission. Three decades later, we are changing it with increasing women in clinical trials globally.

We cannot build equitable healthcare on foundations that were never meant to hold it. The work ahead is re-architecture. Inclusion alone won't get us there. In one of my favorite moments at MedTech Women, a young clinician stood up and said, "We're not asking for seats at the table. We're building new tables." That's what rebuilding infrastructure looks like.

When we reengineer systems around equity, everything improves. Research becomes more accurate, innovation becomes more relevant, and societies become more resilient. Reengineering systems and advancing women's health on a large scale starts with getting institutions to make a change. While it's daunting, it can be done strategically.

How to Get Institutions to Move

Influencing institutions is the slowest, least glamorous part of advancing women's health, but it's also where some of the most consequential shifts happen. Companies get attention. Startups get headlines. But institutions—the World Bank, the WHO, ministries of health, development agencies, the EU Commission, major NGOs—shape the rules, budgets, and priorities that determine what care is available, who receives it, and whose health is considered essential. When institutions change, entire systems move with them.

The challenge isn't that institutions are uninterested in women's health. The challenge is that their priorities are built on outdated assumptions. Women's health is still treated as maternal health, and maternal health is treated as a narrow window of risk, instead of a lifetime economic driver (we already know this from previous chapters). Diseases that disproportionately affect women—autoimmune conditions, chronic pain, pelvic health, cardiovascular disease—remain peripheral in global funding frameworks because the people setting agendas are still operating off old models.

Institutions underfund women's health out of habit. It's why change requires a push from the outside and a pull from the inside. External advocates create pressure. Internal champions create feasibility. Without both, nothing sticks.

I've sat in rooms where a single line in a policy brief—one sentence—altered funding trajectories for years. I've also seen a senior official quietly admit that the data supporting women's health is overwhelming but "doesn't fit this cycle's priorities." These moments are the truth of institutional influence. The system resists change until people inside and out refuse to let it.

> Women's health isn't a "social issue." It's a macroeconomic strategy.

The work begins by finding the right person inside the institution. Not the figurehead who gives speeches but the operator who writes the strategy, shapes the budget, or briefs leadership. These are the people who understand where the institution is rigid, where it's vulnerable, and where it can be moved with the least resistance. When you align with them, you're pushing with someone who can redirect the institution from within.

The most effective way to shift institutional priorities is by reframing women's health as an economic imperative. When institutions see the return on investment, their posture changes. ROI speaks the language they're built to respond to: stability, growth, labor participation, productivity, resilience. Women's health isn't a "social issue." It's a macroeconomic strategy. When you present it that way, budgets start to loosen.

This illustrates why small, successful pilots matter. Institutions rarely take first risks, but they will scale what already works. A cervical cancer screening pilot that increases early detection gives them justification to fund national programs. A diagnostic innovation in Kenya or India demonstrates feasibility for regional expansion. If you want institutions to move, give them something that's already in motion. That's why the capital sources from the previous chapter need to step in early with catalytic capital.

The push–pull dynamic also explains why private institutions stepped in when much of USAID and other strategic US funding was cut in 2025. This created a capital vacuum that needed to be filled quickly in order to avoid healthcare services lapsing for millions of people worldwide. European institutions didn't suddenly develop a new moral stance. They recognized the geopolitical cost of letting women's health systems collapse. Institutional decisions always sit at the crossroads of moral, economic, and political logic. You move institutions when all three begin pointing in the same direction.

Today, private philanthropy is accelerating that alignment (highlighted in Chapter 6). Modern philanthropists write grants and fund catalytic pilots, early-stage innovation, policy experiments, and research that government agencies won't touch yet. Philanthropy is now the R&D engine for institutions. When philanthropists de-risk new models, institutions pay attention. When philanthropists fund out-of-the-box solutions, institutions slowly adopt them. Innovation, evidence, and momentum start outside the system and migrate inward.

Networks and collectives amplify this effect. I'm a founding network member of the Milken Institute Women's Health Network and a member of the Innovation Equity Forum focused on women's health funding architecture building. These groups are strategic leverage points. They bring economic analysis, policy expertise, health innovation, and global partners into the same room. Institutions can dismiss a lone advocate. They can't dismiss a coordinated coalition backed by data, funding, and political weight. Collective influence turns institutional "interest" into institutional obligation.

Yet some of the most effective pressure still comes from people who never planned to be advocates at all. Dense breast legislation passed because patients, clinicians, and small coalitions refused to accept preventable late-stage diagnoses as normal. Supplemental screening coverage expanded because advocates combined stories with data and made the political cost of ignoring the issue too high. Institutions responded because they had no choice.

The pattern is real: institutions follow momentum, not vision.

They respond when public demand, evidence, advocacy, philanthropy, and innovation align so tightly that inaction becomes riskier than change.

The work ahead is about tightening that alignment. Because once institutions move, the scale of impact is unmatched.

Influencing institutions requires understanding the pressure points that move systems. You can pour your energy into the wrong effort for a decade and see nothing shift. But when you learn where decisions originate and where they bottleneck, you can change an entire strategy with one well-timed intervention:

1. FUNDING COMMITTEES

These committees decide what gets resourced. They're anchored in legacy priorities. The fastest way to shift their view is to present women's health as a growth strategy, not a cost center. Budget lines change when the economic situation becomes undeniable.

2. TECHNICAL ADVISORY GROUPS (TAGS)

TAGs shape guidelines, which shape national policies. They care about evidence and feasibility. If you bring data, pilots, and lived reality to a TAG, you can influence entire continents of practice.

3. PROCUREMENT DIVISIONS

Procurement dictates access. They decide which technologies, diagnostics, and treatments get purchased and at what volume. When you shift their cost-benefit assumptions, availability of supply transforms overnight.

4. REGIONAL AND COUNTRY OFFICES

These offices are closer to the ground. They see what works and what doesn't. They're pragmatic, less political, and often more willing to adopt new models if they reduce local burden. If you win over regional leaders, you create scalable proof that institutions can't ignore.

5. LEADERSHIP TRANSITIONS

New leaders bring new priorities. Transition windows are when institutions are most permeable. If you arrive with clarity and solutions while they're still setting strategic agendas, you can embed women's health in the foundation before the bureaucracy solidifies again.

The key is knowing when to apply pressure and when to let the system recalibrate.

> Institutions evolve because the world around them shifts, not because they suddenly become enlightened.

When external advocates provide clarity, evidence, and pressure, internal champions gain leverage. That's the real push–pull dynamic: outside momentum gives inside reformers the power to act.

I've seen a ministry reject a women's diagnostic program for years because of "complexity," only to approve it after a small pilot showed feasibility. I've seen a global NGO deprioritize autoimmune diseases until a coalition presented data showing women's lost productivity was costing economies billions. I've watched institutions reverse-course when public pressure made complacency a reputational risk.

Institutions evolve because the world around them shifts, not because they suddenly become enlightened.

Right now, that shift is accelerating. The economic case for women's health is stronger than ever. The innovation pipeline is expanding. Philanthropy is investing in catalytic, unrestricted work. Advocacy movements are coordinated. Collective networks are aligning strategies. Governments are under pressure to respond to constituents who will no longer accept silence around women's health. All these forces create a tipping point.

Institutions are closer to that tipping point than they've ever been. The data is too strong, the costs too visible, the public too organized, the private sector too engaged, and the global momentum too powerful for institutions to maintain the status quo much longer. But tipping points don't guarantee transformation. They only create opportunities. What turns opportunity into change is sustained pressure—consistent, strategic, coordinated pressure from people who understand the system's weaknesses and refuse to let it retreat into inertia.

Influence can't be limited to policymakers or CEOs. It lives with anyone willing to pick an issue, learn the system, and apply informed pressure. Influence looks like emails, testimonies, meetings, pilots, coalitions, funding, storytelling, research translation, and persistence. Influence looks like refusing to let a necessary change die in committee because no one followed up.

The truth is, institutions aren't impermeable, inflexible, or uninterested. They're just slow, cautious, and overwhelmed. What they need is clarity. What they respond to is momentum. What moves them is pressure combined with solutions.

That's the work. That's the leverage. And that's how we influence institutions that once seemed immovable.

Advocacy Steps

Emerging players—innovators, founders, technologists—are now stepping into advocacy because institutional barriers limit their impact and revenue. When an executive can't get a diagnostic reimbursed because guidelines are outdated, they become a policy actor. When a clinician sees late-stage disease repeatedly, they become an institutional critic. Innovation exposes institutional failure and accelerates institutional reform.

This cross-sector alignment is new, powerful, and exactly what women's health has lacked. Because institutional change accelerates when internal frustration meets external momentum.

Advocacy is not the same as noise. Effective advocacy is targeted, persistent, specific, and strategic. It focuses on one ask at a time. It follows up. It knows who has real power. It brings evidence and emotion in equal measure. It recognizes that lawmakers and institutional leaders often care but don't know enough to act confidently.

For many, advocacy feels intimidating because they imagine policy work as something reserved for experts. You don't need political fluency. You need precision. You need to say: here's the problem, here's the evidence, here's the solution, and here's what we need you to do. For those who want to move beyond awareness and influence policy, the process usually follows a series of practical steps that can take you from awareness to advocacy.

1. **Pick your lane.** You can't fix everything. Choose the issue you're willing to carry.
2. **Learn who holds actual authority.** Titles mislead. Influence lives with the people writing the drafts, shaping the budgets, and briefing leadership.
3. **Build a small coalition.** Movements scale because small groups refuse to quit.
4. **Pair lived experience with data.** Narrative drives emotion. Evidence drives action.
5. **Be specific in every ask.** "Improve women's health" is meaningless. "Mandate secondary screening coverage for women with dense breasts" is actionable.
6. **Follow up relentlessly.** Systems move when someone refuses to let the issue fade.
7. **Recognize your power.** Institutions rely on public disengagement. Your voice is a disruption.

Advocacy reshapes political safety. Institutions respond when silence becomes riskier than change. Grassroots power proves this. Crowdfunding, patient coalitions, and small advocacy groups have passed legislation, changed payer coverage, and elevated issues institutions overlooked for decades. They remind everyone that institutional influence is cumulative.

Several of my examples are US focused because my personal voting power is in the US, but this same model is replicated around the world. From India to the UK, South Africa, and Mexico, laws and standards have changed because of advocacy framed correctly.

I'm part of the leadership team of Women's Health Advocates (WHA), and it's a clear example of how disciplined, sustained advocacy can move policy in systems that rarely prioritize women. It was built with a clear thesis: women's health policy fails because of a lack of disciplined execution. Founded by leaders who spent years navigating gaps in diagnostics, reimbursement, and regulatory pathways, WHA positioned itself as a strategic policy engine rather than a grassroots protest movement.

Its approach is structured and replicable: identify a narrowly defined policy failure, compile clinical and economic evidence, build bipartisan legislative champions, activate directly impacted patients with coordinated messaging, and pursue incremental wins at the state level before scaling federally.

Rather than chasing headlines, single-issue wins, or broad "awareness" campaigns, WHA focuses on precision and keeping women's health embedded in broader healthcare legislation where real funding and enforcement decisions are made. It translates complex policy into clear, actionable positions for lawmakers, reducing friction for decision-makers who want to act but lack time or expertise. It builds coalitions across clinicians, medical societies, briefing regulators, payers, patients, and policymakers to move from problem recognition to statutory change. It shows up year after year, across administrations and budget negotiations, ensuring women's health doesn't disappear when political attention shifts.

Through this disciplined strategy, WHA has helped advance endometriosis research and coverage, expand coverage discussions around secondary imaging, and elevate women's diagnostic equity into mainstream policy conversations. It helped elevate postpartum depression from an acknowledged problem to a funded policy priority, supporting federal programs for screening, treatment, and workforce training. When women's health benefits were politically vulnerable, it played a role in protecting no-cost access to preventive services during regulatory and legislative challenges.

Its real achievement is demonstrating that when advocacy is structured, data-driven, and persistent, women's health policy can move from fragmented efforts to national standards. It also shows that when a small group of aligned individuals organize around a specific cause, the voice of the collective is more powerful than the individual.

Their impact underscores a critical lesson in institutional influence: policy change rarely comes from dramatic moments. It comes from being relentless, credible, and impossible to ignore. Women's Health Advocates relies on endurance. In systems built to outlast outrage, endurance is power.

And that raises an uncomfortable truth. For every partnership that drives real progress, many more fail because the structure behind the partnership was flawed from the start.

Why Partnerships Fail

Beyond the usual "they" didn't do their job well enough, we need to be far more honest about why so many partnerships fail. They don't fail because the vision is wrong. They fail because power is never shared. They fail because institutions expect women to show gratitude instead of leadership. They fail because timelines are unrealistic, budgets are underfunded, and "stakeholder engagement" means a single meeting where the real decision-makers aren't present. They fail because egos are louder than insights. They fail because no one wants to redesign the model after early signs showed it wasn't working.

Sometimes they fail because of changes in the political landscape.

Jhpiego, an NGO spun out of Johns Hopkins University, introduced HERhealthEQ to Sika Kaboré, the First Lady of Burkina Faso who founded the Kimi Foundation during the UN General Assembly meetings in 2018. HERhealthEQ partnered with Kimi Foundation via Jhpiego and donated two pieces of equipment for cervical cancer detection and treatment. And the partnership worked—until it didn't. Because the organization was founded and led by the First Lady of the country, we lost control of the equipment, access to information, and follow-up when political factions changed and caused political strife in the country. Our main contacts were no longer in the positions of power, and we didn't have contact with the clinic that received the equipment. To this day, we don't know if the equipment is still being used.

No single organization was at fault. The fault was collective, in how we set up the partnership model in the first place.

It was a great lesson for a small NGO to learn: don't partner with NGOs that can change dramatically based on the political landscape, and ensure we have the contact information for all the receivers of the equipment so that we can always have direct communication with them. We have partnered with the support of other governments since then, but they are in programs that will continue regardless of the administration.

Partnerships succeed when they confront these complexities head-on instead of pretending everyone is aligned. Women's health is full of people who believe deeply in the mission but work inside systems that resist change. When you understand that dynamic, you stop assuming lack of progress is the result of incompetence or apathy.

Real partnership also acknowledges that women's health does not progress in isolation. It sits inside political systems, economic conditions, cultural structures, and global power dynamics. You can't "partner" your way out of these realities with a memorandum of understanding and a project plan. You must navigate them honestly. That means accepting that some institutions are slow because their incentives make them slow, some governments hesitate because every decision has political consequences, and some donors cling to outdated strategies because that's what their boards expect. It means recognizing that communities may carry generations of skepticism because outsiders have repeatedly promised progress and delivered disappointment.

> Investors, philanthropists, and governments that once treated LMICs as "recipients" are now learning that these regions hold the innovation playbook the rest of the world needs.

Partnership that works is partnership that evolves. It's not rigid, precious, or defensive. It knows when to pivot. It knows when to hand over the reins. It knows when to slow down, speed up, or redesign the entire strategy because the context requires it. Adaptability is the oxygen that keeps a partnership alive.

Investors, philanthropists, and governments that once treated LMICs as "recipients" are now learning that these regions hold the innovation playbook the rest of the world needs. Middle-income countries across Africa, Asia, and Latin America are designing cost-effective health solutions that outperform high-income counterparts, precisely because they're built for scale and real-world constraints. Task shifting in community health? Born in LMICs. Mobile-first healthcare models? Born in LMICs. Community data systems? Born in LMICs. These are the innovations that create durable impact because they emerge from constraints rather than theory. And when we partner correctly, we amplify those ideas.

True partnership means we stop overlooking those models and start elevating them. True partnership centers women's expertise, invests in locally created solutions, and treats community voices as the foundation.

Men Have a Role to Play in Women's Health

True inclusion requires sponsorship, not just presence. Women need allies—real allies, not performative ones—to challenge outdated norms that limit innovation.

Sometimes the most powerful form of partnership is simply asking, "Who should be leading this instead of me?" That means releasing ownership of ideas, spotlight, and credit. It means putting the right people in charge, even when funders or institutions expect someone with a Western resume to run the show. This is uncomfortable for people who are rewarded for visibility, but progress depends on discomfort. Staying comfortable is how we got here.

What's equally important is that innovating for women never means speaking for them. It means clearing the path so they can speak for themselves. That's where allies play a crucial role. Allies create access, not narratives. They support, not overshadow. They ensure women aren't the lone voice in a room navigating power dynamics that shouldn't exist in the first place. They help normalize women's expertise as a driving force, not a special case. They make sure women are heard. They make room. They redirect credit when ideas get misattributed. They ensure the burden of fixing systemic issues doesn't fall exclusively on the people harmed by those issues.

"Speaking for women" misses the point. Women don't need proxies. They need platforms. They need allies who open doors and step back, not take the microphone. The most effective allies amplify women's expertise, make room for them in decision-making spaces, and challenge systems that suppress their influence.

There is a moment I often think about when talking to men who want to support women's health but don't know how to do it without overstepping. I was speaking on a panel at AdvaMed's MedTech conference in October 2025, where the majority of decision-makers were men. During the question-and-answer session after our discussion, Max Horton, the Director of Global Inclusion and Belonging at Smith & Nephew, stood up and asked a question that froze the room:

> *"How do I stand up for women without speaking for them?"*

You could feel the sincerity behind it. He wasn't asking how to become a male savior. He was trying to figure out how to use his privilege without abusing it. That's the inflection point men need to reach: understanding that allyship isn't performance and it's not silence. It's using influence to open the doors women have been pounding on for decades, while making sure women walk through those doors themselves and speak in their own voices.

If more men asked that question, we would accelerate progress overnight. Because men still hold most of the institutional power—politically, financially, and structurally. Women have the expertise while men often have the leverage. When those two forces collaborate respectfully, change happens faster. And when women are forced to navigate systems designed to keep them out, progress slows to a crawl. Respect is the accelerator; paternalism is the brake.

At a small, private gathering of healthcare executives in 2024, a male participant who wishes to remain anonymous told me he was afraid to advocate for women because he didn't want to speak over them. That's the right fear. But the answer is strategy, not silence.

- Men can mentor, sponsor, and elevate women without centering themselves.
- Men can step back so women can speak, and step forward when institutional bias needs to be challenged.
- Men can redirect opportunities.
- Men can make introductions that accelerate progress.
- Men can remove barriers.
- Men can refuse to participate in panels or leadership spaces that

exclude women.

- Men can advocate for women's advancement behind closed doors where many of the real decisions in global health are made. That is partnership.

Men have a role. Women have a voice. When both are aligned and working from the same playbook, structural change stops being conceptual and starts being operational.

The strongest teams are embedding women into every stage of innovation: problem identification, drafting requirements, prototyping, human factors testing, study design, commercial strategy, and market validation. They're redesigning workflows to ensure women's input isn't optional or "advisory" but central to decision-making. And they're integrating equity into their key performance metrics, treating it as a measurable driver of product performance rather than soft value.

Men have a role. Women have a voice. When both are aligned and working from the same playbook, structural change stops being conceptual and starts being operational.

This matters because innovation thrives in environments where assumptions are questioned.

The dynamic plays out across industries. When women contribute to design, everything from ergonomics to workflows to outcomes improves. When women contribute to engineering, products work across more contexts. When women contribute to clinical strategy, trials become more accurate. When women contribute to leadership, companies make more responsible, longer-horizon decisions.

Respectful Collaboration

This chapter—and this entire section of the book—ends on this point for a reason: nothing in women's health moves without collaboration rooted in respect. Not innovation. Not investment. Not policy. Not scale. Everything we've covered so far only works if partnerships are built with intention, humility, and shared power.

That brings us back to Horton. His question at the MedTech conference captures the tension at the heart of global women's health. Allyship means standing beside women and using influence to remove barriers, amplify women's expertise, and ensure their voices are heard directly rather than translated or replaced.

Women need partners, not a new generation of gatekeepers. Women need the resources to build the solutions they know will work, not solutions handed to them. Women need donors who trust them, not donors who "empower" them. Women need institutions to design with them, not for them.

Partnerships done well are the opposite of charity, saviorism, and the old global health model that assumed ideas flowed in one direction. Partnership is shared ownership, shared responsibility, shared success, and shared credit. It moves progress from something imposed to something co-created and sustainable.

Here's how we honor the core truth of women's health: women already know what they need. They have always known. Whether we are investors, innovators, policymakers, clinicians, or advocates, our job is to build with them and follow their lead, not speak over them or design around them.

Partnership, not patronizing. Co-creation, not control. Collaboration, not ego.

If we can get that right, that's how you create lasting infrastructure.

Chapter 7 Takeaways

- **PARTNERSHIP MUST HAVE SHARED POWER.** LASTING PROGRESS IN WOMEN'S HEALTH HAPPENS WHEN WOMEN AND COMMUNITIES ARE TREATED AS CO-ARCHITECTS, NOT IMPLEMENTATION ARMS.
- **INSTITUTIONS DON'T MOVE ON GOODWILL ALONE.** CHANGE HAPPENS WHEN ADVOCACY, EVIDENCE, ECONOMIC LOGIC, AND INTERNAL CHAMPIONS ALIGN.
- **THE STRONGEST PARTNERSHIPS ARE BUILT ON TRUST, LOCAL OWNERSHIP, AND ADAPTABILITY.** SOLUTIONS LAST WHEN THEY EVOLVE WITH CONTEXT, DISTRIBUTE CREDIT, AND SHIFT POWER TO THE PEOPLE CLOSEST TO THE PROBLEM.
- **ALLYSHIP MATTERS WHEN IT CREATES ACCESS WITHOUT TAKING CONTROL.** THE ROLE OF PARTNERS, ESPECIALLY MEN AND INSTITUTIONS, IS TO OPEN DOORS, SHARE INFLUENCE, AND MAKE SURE WOMEN LEAD IN THEIR OWN VOICES.

PART III: **NOW ACT**

At some point we have to move past diagnosing the failures of the system and how to redesign them into how to lead differently. We have enough evidence now to say with confidence that organizations can scale and stay values driven. They can maintain mission integrity while delivering strong ROI. They can include women without apologizing for it, and they can center equity without becoming "charity." They can build businesses that prove a simple idea: doing good for women is good for business.

We, collectively as the women's health industry, need to stop only talking, planning, and diagnosing the problem. We need to start acting on all the talks, plans, and diagnoses we know to be true. It's time to make changes and treat women's health as the good business we know it is.

Then the real question isn't whether it's possible. The real question is: *Why isn't everyone doing it already?*

Chapter 8: **Your Organization**

One of the most harmful myths in business is that integrating purpose or social mission makes a company "soft." Women's health has often fallen into that category. Purpose is about architecture—the structural decisions that define how a business builds, operates, and grows, and who it serves.

Purpose creates clarity. Companies lose their soul when they don't know who they serve. Purpose anchors the organization, ensuring that product decisions align with mission, hiring decisions align with culture, partnership decisions align with values, and investment decisions align with long-term strategy.

That alignment is what allows companies to scale without drifting into incoherence.

Purpose attracts better talent. The market has shifted. Younger workers, especially women, will not trade their values for a paycheck. They want to work for organizations that matter. Companies that center women's health, equity, and mission-driven innovation have a competitive advantage in recruiting.

Great talent doesn't want to work for companies that treat mission as garnish. They want companies where the mission drives decisions.

Purpose builds better products. When companies build with women in mind, from clinical trials to usability to leadership, the end result is a product that serves more people with greater accuracy.

Purpose is not a PR exercise. Companies that scale with soul do something simple: they build giving, impact, and social purpose into the core business model. Not only is this possible; it's becoming expected.

It's differentiation, not weakness. Purpose is economically rational when built into the business engine, not bolted on after the fact.

Scaling Without Losing Soul

There's a moment in every organization's life—whether a startup, a global NGO, a Fortune 50 giant, or a scrappy medtech team still working out of borrowed office space—when the executives look up and realize something terrifying: growth is here. It's exhilarating, but it's also a stress test. It tests systems, values, leadership, culture, mission, and the promises an organization makes about who it exists to serve. Here's the uncomfortable truth many leaders learn too late: growth doesn't change your identity. Growth exposes your identity.

Growth and values aren't opposites. They're accelerants if you build the company right.

We don't need hypotheticals or wishful thinking. I want to start this chapter off with some examples to ground our understanding in reality. Some are household names, others are organizations quietly reshaping markets from the inside. What they all have in common is this: they didn't lose their soul on the way up. If anything, their commitment to women became their competitive advantage.

GROWTH BY PUTTING WOMEN IN THE ROOM

Insulet, the company behind the Omnipod insulin pump, is often talked about in terms of engineering and innovation. But the real story, the one leaders should pay attention to, is what happened when women were elevated into meaningful executive roles. When women stepped into operational, strategic, and leadership positions, Insulet didn't become "softer" or "less focused." It became more competitive.

And the results weren't incremental. Under CEO Shacey Petrovic's leadership from 2016 to 2022, Insulet grew revenue from roughly $240 million to more than $1.1 billion while launching new generations of its Omnipod insulin delivery platform. The company also expanded globally, increasing its market capitalization to more than $15 billion. All because women brought the perspective, discipline, strategic clarity, and lived experience that had been missing. Women understood the invisible friction points in healthcare decision-making, in household budgeting, in consumer trust, in product usability. When those perspectives influence the design, marketing, and commercialization strategies, you serve more people, and you retain them.

That's not mission drift. That's strategy.

Insulet didn't scale despite bringing women into leadership. It scaled *because* of it.

WHEN WOMEN'S HEALTH ISN'T AN AFTERTHOUGHT

GE Healthcare has many divisions, but none has been more consistently powerful—or more financially successful—than its women's health and imaging division. Notice that it's not a side initiative. It's not tucked beneath a philanthropic arm. It's not a CSR add-on. It's one of the company's largest divisions.

And why wouldn't it be? Women live longer. Women interact with the healthcare system more frequently across their lifespan. Women's diagnostics, from ultrasounds to DEXA scanners, are recurring, predictable, high-value services. When a company builds an entire division around this reality, it's intelligent economics.

GE Healthcare has scaled globally while keeping its women's health mission at the center of the business model. It gained dominance by focusing on women. This should be the obvious path for every healthcare company, but it isn't. That gap is the opportunity.

THE POWER OF CARVING OUT A WOMEN'S HEALTH IDENTITY

Merck's spin-off Organon created the only global pharmaceutical company dedicated to women's health at scale. That decision strengthened Merck's brand. And for Organon, the mandate was clear: build a company grounded in science, market reach, and pipeline development that addresses conditions women face.

Organon's existence proves an important point: women's health is not a niche. Women are not an edge case. When a legacy company chooses to focus deeply on women, it differentiates itself, and the market rewards that.

PROOF THAT "WOMEN'S HEALTH COMPANY" IS NOT A LIMITING LABEL

Between 2004 and 2013, I spent more than nine formative years at Hologic and developed my love of women's health. It's a company that never pretended to be something else. It didn't tiptoe around the word "women." It didn't worry that focusing on women made it smaller. Instead, Hologic built—and continues to build—a global business rooted in women's health technologies, diagnostics, and equity.

The result? Strong financial performance, market respect, dominance in key screening categories, some of the most impactful global initiatives in cervical cancer detection and breast health, and a reputation for reliability that money can't buy.

Hologic scaled without losing soul because soul was hardwired into who it is.

Scale with soul isn't just a healthcare phenomenon. We see the same pattern in consumer goods, especially in companies that understand who their customers are.

CVS Health, for example, made a series of deliberate decisions that signaled women's health is core to its long-term strategy: removing tobacco, improving access to reproductive health products, investing in maternal health initiatives, and expanding care models that serve women as primary household health managers. Yes, these decisions were values driven. They were also profitable. They strengthened customer loyalty and positioned CVS as a trusted brand, especially among women who are often the healthcare gatekeepers for families.

Other consumer packaged goods players like Procter & Gamble, Unilever, and L'Oréal have long understood that centering women is a competitive necessity. Their strongest product lines, most loyal customer segments, and most consistent revenue streams come from products designed with women in mind. These companies didn't scale because they ignored women; they scaled because they couldn't afford to.

Organon built purpose into its product pipeline. Hologic built purpose into screening access. GE Healthcare built purpose into imaging innovation. Insulet built purpose into leadership representation and patient experience. CVS Health built purpose into access and trust. These choices expanded their markets.

The message is clear: companies that bet on women win.

Women in Leadership Drive Performance

For anyone who still believes focusing on women or having women in leadership is a "nice to have," the data should end the debate. It's about returns, not ideology.

BOARDS WITH WOMEN OUTPERFORM BOARDS WITHOUT THEM

Multiple global studies have found that companies with gender-diverse leadership outperform their peers. Global analyses from the Peterson Institute and Morgan Stanley Capital International (MSCI) have linked female board representation to higher returns on equity and stronger financial performance.

MSCI's analysis found that US companies with three or more women on their boards experienced median earnings-per-share gains of 37 percent over a five-year period, compared to an 8 percent decline for companies with no female directors.

That's not a rounding error. When women lead, companies win.

DIVERSE LEADERSHIP EQUALS BETTER PROFITABILITY

McKinsey's 2020 report found that companies in the top quartile for gender diversity on their executive teams were 25 percent more likely to financially outperform peers. That number has grown from 15 percent in 2014, meaning the advantage of gender-diverse leadership is intensifying.

Bloomberg Intelligence adds another layer: companies with greater gender diversity deliver higher annual returns and show less volatility, especially in emerging markets, where companies with the most female board members were 2 to 6 percent less volatile than the least-diverse competitors. That's a massive delta. Emerging markets are where volatility is expected, yet diversity stabilizes performance.

Volatility is expensive. Diversity is economical.

If you're an investor or executive who says you want stability, resilience, and long-term value creation, the data is effectively shouting the answer. Women in leadership are strategic assets. The math speaks for itself.

Women in leadership are strategic assets. The math speaks for itself.

LESS EXCESSIVE RISK-TAKING

High-performing organizations don't avoid risk. They understand risk. The goal is intelligent, not zero, volatility. Companies must invest, acquire, innovate, pivot, and place bets. But too many organizations take the wrong risks because their leadership teams look the same, think the same, and reinforce one another's blind spots. Women change the strategy.

Study after study shows that gender-diverse boards are associated with less aggressive, unbalanced risk-taking. That doesn't mean women are risk averse. It means women take calculated risks. There's a difference.

All-male boards, especially when dominated by a certain machismo style of leadership, tend to overweigh aggressive expansion strategies, pursue questionable acquisitions, or push overleveraged financial structures. The 2008 financial crisis and countless corporate collapses are evidence of how easily confidence without counterbalance turns into catastrophe.

During financial, reputational, and operational crises, boards with women demonstrate higher resilience. Women tend to approach problems holistically, analyzing second-order effects and considering downstream impacts.

Women add counterweight, not to kill deals, but to refine them.

BETTER ACQUISITION AND INVESTMENT DECISIONS

Acquisitions fail at staggering rates—between 70 and 90 percent depending on the industry—usually because assumptions were flawed, diligence was rushed, synergies were overestimated, or leadership failed to consider integration realities.

Boards with more women demonstrate stronger performance in

acquisition strategy. They ask different questions:

- Does this acquisition expand actual strategic value?
- Are we buying into a cultural mismatch?
- Is the revenue projection real or wishful thinking?
- Are we investing in growth or ego?

It's about pattern recognition, not personality. Women challenge groupthink, which has historically destroyed more corporate value than any external competitor.

Groupthink is what better governance prevents, and women are the interceding factor.

Governance Is Better When Women Are at the Table

One of the most consistent findings in corporate research over the last twenty years is that women improve governance.

Consistently. Measurably. Repeatedly.

BETTER MONITORING, BETTER DISCIPLINE

Boards with women have better meeting attendance, stronger committee engagement, and more rigorous oversight. That matters because good governance is about discipline. The blocking and tackling of corporate leadership: financial oversight, audits, risk reviews, compliance monitoring, and long-term strategy evaluation are what create better companies.

Women show up. Women dig in. Women monitor.

Studies have found that female directors spend more time preparing for meetings, ask more direct questions in the boardroom, and challenge assumptions more frequently. This leads to fewer "rubber stamp" decisions and more meaningful discussion about strategic direction.

That's the backbone of corporate governance: people who are willing to interrogate decisions, not just nod along.

FEWER FINANCIAL RESTATEMENTS

Financial restatements are costly. They erode trust, drag down stock prices, and often signal deeper issues in internal controls. Companies with at least one woman on the board experience fewer restatements. It's the natural result of better oversight.

Restatements typically arise from sloppy processes, lack of diligence, misaligned incentives, overconfidence, or insufficient internal controls. Diverse boards interrupt those patterns. They force companies to slow down, double-check assumptions, and ensure accuracy.

If you care about investor trust—and every leader should—diversity is non-negotiable.

STRONGER ESG PERFORMANCE

Environmental, social, and governance isn't about political ideology; it's about risk. Companies with poor ESG structures face higher volatility, higher regulatory exposure, and higher reputational risk. Companies with stronger ESG indicators demonstrate resilience, improved stakeholder trust, and better long-term performance.

Studies have found that companies with greater female representation on corporate boards tend to demonstrate stronger environmental performance, including lower greenhouse gas emissions, improved energy management, and better stewardship of natural resources such as water.

These are operational improvements, not feel-good stories. They reduce input costs, strengthen compliance, and signal long-term stability to investors who understand risk.

And the logic behind it is straightforward: companies with leaders who reflect the world are better at understanding how the world is changing.

Women don't make companies "nicer." Women make companies smarter.

The question isn't whether to center women in business and leadership. It's how to stay committed to it as the organization grows.

CROSS-INDUSTRY EXAMPLES: **WHEN PURPOSE DRIVES PERFORMANCE**

Healthcare isn't the only sector that demonstrates how mission-proofing and staying core to your customers establishes market dominance. The companies that integrate purpose early and operationalize it are consistently the ones that scale with stability.

- **UNILEVER: PURPOSE-LED BUSINESS AT GLOBAL SCALE.** UNDER PAUL POLMAN AND LATER LEADERS, UNILEVER PROVED THAT SUSTAINABILITY AND SOCIAL PURPOSE CAN DRIVE PROFITABILITY. THEIR PURPOSE-DRIVEN BRANDS (INCLUDING DOVE, LIFEBUOY, AND SUNSILK) CONSISTENTLY OUTPERFORMED FINANCIALLY. THIS WAS ALIGNMENT, NOT MAGIC. CLEANER SUPPLY CHAINS, STRONGER CONSUMER TRUST, REDUCED RISK, AND LONG-TERM THINKING DID THE WORK.
- **PROCTER & GAMBLE: DESIGN FOR REAL HOUSEHOLDS, NOT HYPOTHETICAL ONES.** P&G'S STRONGEST CATEGORIES HAVE SUCCEEDED BECAUSE THE COMPANY HAS LONG INVESTED IN UNDERSTANDING WOMEN AS THE PRIMARY DECISION-MAKERS ACROSS HOUSEHOLD GOODS. THEIR INNOVATION PATHWAYS ARE GROUNDED IN LIVED EXPERIENCE: USABILITY, PRICE, PSYCHOLOGICAL TRUST, DAILY ROUTINES.

- **L'ORÉAL: WOMEN IN LEADERSHIP EQUALS MARKET MASTERY.** L'ORÉAL'S CONSISTENT FINANCIAL DOMINANCE ISN'T ACCIDENTAL. IT STEMS FROM BUILDING A LEADERSHIP PIPELINE WHERE WOMEN CAN AND DO RISE TO SENIOR ROLES. THAT REPRESENTATION SHAPES PRODUCT LINES, MARKETING INTEGRITY, MERGERS AND ACQUISITIONS DECISIONS, AND GLOBAL STRATEGY.

These companies don't brand themselves as "women's companies," yet they win because they understand women drive the global consumer market.

Mission-Proofing

Here's the inflection point leaders must confront: Are you willing to grow in a way that honors the people you exist to serve?

Scale will force that question. Growth will expose everything: culture, governance, leadership, operations, priorities, blind spots. The companies in this chapter didn't get lucky. They didn't stumble into ethical growth. They made repeated, disciplined choices to align mission and performance.

Scaling without losing soul isn't about perfection. It's about direction. Most importantly, it's about understanding that the biggest growth markets in the world are not the markets companies have historically served. The future is women. The future is equity. The future is markets previously overlooked because they were dismissed as "too small," "too complex," or "too unfamiliar"—including globally.

Every leader who reaches scale faces the same tension: the company grows faster than the culture can keep up. It's not enough to believe in mission-driven growth. Leaders need the operating system to execute it. A set of decisions, trade-offs, and design choices, often made quietly, internally, and long before a company hits the public radar.

Some companies do this instinctively. Others learn the hard way, usually after they've already drifted. But the organizations that scale well share a pattern: they build structures that prevent them from forgetting who they are. They create guardrails to prevent drift.

Guardrail #1: Protect your core user. If you lose clarity about who you serve, growth becomes chaotic. If women are your core users, build systems around them, not around abstract market averages.

Guardrail #2: Never make leadership homogeneous. Homogeneous leadership is the fastest path to strategic blindness. If everyone in the room thinks alike, you're making fast decisions. You're not making good ones. Those are rarely the same.

Guardrail #3: Mission must be a filter, not a tagline. If your mission can't veto revenue, it isn't a mission. If equity can't override speed, it isn't equity. If purpose can't shape strategy, it isn't purpose.

Guardrail #4: Expand slowly, but intentionally. Companies that try to become everything to everyone lose meaning. Scaling with soul means expanding in ways that deepen mission, not dilute it.

Guardrail #5: Build products for real constraints. This means designing for access, affordability, usability, and cultural context, not for hypothetical optimal conditions.

These structures aren't glamorous. They don't get press releases. They don't trend on social media. But they anchor a company during moments when growth threatens to pull it off mission.

Values disappear when they live only in slide decks and speeches. They survive when they're hardwired into every operational layer of the company. Leaders who successfully scale with soul understand that mission isn't self-sustaining. It needs reinforcement:

EMBED MISSION IN DECISION-MAKING TOOLS

This includes R&D prioritization frameworks, product roadmaps, partnership evaluation processes, budget allocation cycles, strategic OKRs, and talent promotion criteria. If none of those include direct questions about equity, users, and impact, then mission becomes aspirational instead of operational.

Companies like Hologic and Organon didn't succeed because they "care" about women. They succeed because their internal operating systems force them to consider women in every strategic decision. Mission is the software the company runs on.

CREATE INTERNAL RED LINES

Companies often avoid this because it feels limiting, but red lines actually create freedom. They prevent values from drifting by making the boundaries explicit.

For example:

- We don't commercialize products that haven't been validated in the populations we claim to serve.
- We don't acquire companies whose values contradict our core mission.
- We don't pursue growth models that undermine access or equity.
- We don't build leadership teams that fail to reflect the people we serve.

These red lines don't slow growth; they sharpen it. Red lines prevent expensive mistakes, protect brand identity, and help teams make faster decisions because the parameters are already defined.

PROTECT THE USER AT THE CENTER

One reason equity-centered companies outperform is because they design with clarity. They know exactly who they serve and why. They do not build products for "everyone," because "everyone" is the death of focus.

Insulet focused on the lived experience of insulin users. Hologic focused on women who need diagnostics. GE Healthcare focused on imaging pathways that disproportionately affect women. CVS focused on the real healthcare decision-makers in households. When a company knows its user intimately, scale becomes a precision exercise, not a guessing game. Mission-driven companies lose their way when they start designing for abstractions.

MAKE WOMEN A DEFINED USE CASE, NOT A SUB-CATEGORY

Here's where many organizations fail. They treat women as an afterthought—as a "segment" instead of the core. Companies that scale well design studies that include women proportionally, create usability tests with female-led panels, prioritize conditions that predominantly affect women, and build products for a spectrum of ages, bodies, and life stages.

They don't "shrink it and pink it." They build for reality.

RUN INNOVATION THROUGH EQUITY STRESS TESTS

Before launch, companies with strong mission alignment ask:

- Does this product work for all the women we claim it will?
- Did we include diverse testers?
- Will the price point exclude the people who need it most?
- Are we assuming that access is equal across all regions?
- Does the distribution model reinforce or reduce inequity?
- Does the user journey reflect real constraints women face?

These questions prevent costly failures. They force companies to see blind spots before they hit the market. We can't consider this "extra." It's risk mitigation.

AVOID THE "SCALE EQUALS STANDARDIZATION" TRAP

Standardization is appealing to executives because it feels efficient. But in women's health, standardization often creates blind spots.

Global examples make this clear:

- A cervical screening device that works perfectly in Boston may fail in Kenya if it requires consumables that aren't available, or if women must travel long distances to clinics.
- A digital app designed by urban developers will fail in rural India if it assumes uninterrupted internet or smartphone access.
- A maternal health solution built for high-income hospitals will collapse in LMIC settings without task-shifting, nurse-led workflows, or community-level support.

Scaling for all means you adapt your innovation without diluting your mission.

Culture as Strategy

Ask any executive who has lived through hyper-growth. The real risk is losing culture, not money. Once culture erodes, everything else gets harder.

Representation is culture's first line of defense. But here's the key: inclusion only works when it's operational, not symbolic. Adding one woman to a ten-person team won't magically shift outcomes. Asking her to "represent all women" is unrealistic and irresponsible. Inclusion becomes real when it's designed into the process. Real representation means women are decision-makers, budget owners, product architects, researchers, board members, revenue leaders, and profit-and-loss owners.

Companies must stop confusing visibility with influence. A woman featured on a website is not the same as a woman at the table where decisions are made. A women's employee resource group is not valuable unless leadership listens to it and integrates its insights into the development pipeline. Inviting women into key meetings without giving them decision-making authority is performance, not inclusion.

Companies that successfully scale with soul know that culture is set by who holds power, in every area of business. It's infrastructure.

Build a culture that rewards truth-telling. Mission breaks when teams stop speaking up. When dissent becomes uncomfortable. When overly confident executives dominate the room. When questioning assumptions is treated as disloyalty.

High-performing companies do the opposite. They institutionalize truth-telling.

That looks like encouraging hard questions in leadership meetings, rewarding people who spot risks early, creating psychological safety for employees to surface issues, and giving teams the autonomy to push back when mission is at risk.

Make equity non-negotiable in internal policies. Flexible work, parental leave, leadership pathways, mentorship, pay equity enforcement, and grievance systems that actually work should never be "HR perks." They're strategic levers. Women don't stay or rise in organizations that treat them as replaceable. And companies that bleed female talent can never claim to be scaling with integrity.

Equity is not a benefit. It's a retention strategy. And retention is cheaper than recruitment by a factor of ten.

When companies don't build these systems, they drift. They start chasing short-term wins at the expense of long-term value. They hire speed over alignment. They lose their soul in increments, often without noticing.

Equity is not a benefit. It's a retention strategy.

The Power of Representation

Representation and purpose change outcomes. Period.

When women lead clinical trials, female participation rises by nearly 20 percent. When women sit on hospital boards, budgets shift toward community health. When women head research labs, funding expands to cover neglected conditions like autoimmune disease, menopause, and chronic pain.

As Mary Barra, CEO of General Motors said at the 2019 World Economic Forum, "Diversity is not a nice-to-have. It's a must-have for businesses that want to compete and win."

Representation works because it changes what's visible. It diversifies decision-making, broadens empathy, and aligns priorities with reality.

Chapter 8 Takeaways

- **PURPOSE IS STRATEGY.** COMPANIES THAT BUILD MISSION INTO THE BUSINESS MODEL ATTRACT BETTER TALENT, BUILD BETTER PRODUCTS, AND SCALE WITH GREATER CLARITY AND DISCIPLINE.
- **COMPANIES THAT CENTER WOMEN EXPAND THEIR MARKET.** WOMEN'S HEALTH IS A LARGE, DURABLE, AND UNDERLEVERAGED GROWTH OPPORTUNITY.
- **WOMEN IN LEADERSHIP IMPROVE PERFORMANCE, GOVERNANCE, AND RESILIENCE.** MORE DIVERSE LEADERSHIP LEADS TO BETTER DECISIONS, STRONGER OVERSIGHT, SMARTER RISK-TAKING, AND BETTER LONG-TERM RETURNS.
- **SCALING WITHOUT LOSING SOUL REQUIRES OPERATIONAL GUARDRAILS.** MISSION, EQUITY, AND REPRESENTATION MUST BE EMBEDDED INTO DECISIONS, LEADERSHIP, PRODUCT DESIGN, AND CULTURE, OR GROWTH WILL EXPOSE THE GAPS.

Chapter 9: **The Future**

The future shouldn't be an abstract idea. It's a set of choices being made right now. And for the first time in history, the world is waking up to the most underleveraged truth in global development: when women are healthy, educated, empowered, and leading, societies become stronger, more resilient, and more prosperous.

And the future is here. I've seen it in person while speaking to engineering students at my alma mater Boston University's College of Engineering in January 2026. At an optional lecture the first week into the spring semester, I gave a talk titled "Advancing Women's Health: The Industry and Opportunities." The room was filled with 75 students, both men and women, who chose to attend. Afterward, more than 30 students lined up to speak with me. Every single one of them told me about what they were working on in women's health and asked me what else they could do. They ranged from sophomores to graduate students and they all wanted to do more, innovate further, and solve problems they've seen firsthand. They're the next generation of leaders who have been watching those of us doing the work for the last twenty-five years.

The greatest shift in the future is what happens when women are healthy across their entire lifespan. Healthy girls become educated women. Educated women join the workforce. Working women innovate, vote, lead, and reinvest in their families. Women in midlife stay in leadership roles because perimenopause and menopause are treated with evidence-based care rather than silence. Aging women remain active because they receive screening and treatment for osteoporosis, cardiovascular disease, diabetes, and cancer as standard care. When women are healthy, everyone benefits: healthier children, stronger families, more stable societies, more productive economies, and more resilience during crises. The multiplying effect is real and measurable.

> When women are healthy, everyone benefits: healthier children, stronger families, more stable societies, more productive economies, and more resilience during crises.

This isn't a fantasy of what could be. It's a reflection of what I've already seen happen in the places that have chosen to invest in women. And it's a warning to the places that still believe gender equity is optional. Countries that fail to invest in women will fall behind economically, politically, socially, and health-wise. There is no scenario in which a nation sidelines half its population and competes effectively on the global stage.

You wouldn't build a road with intentional potholes, and we shouldn't build societies that miss the health of half the population. Both are infrastructure.

I've seen us shift from thinking of women's health as only bikini medicine, to leveraging entire financial categories around it. There are more reports and proof-points, conferences to discuss it, innovative ideas and companies, and leaders willing to step into the space than I've seen in my past twenty-five years.

The future belongs to the places that recognize women as economic engines, leaders, innovators, and central players in global well-being. And it belongs to the institutions—public, private, and philanthropic—that choose to modernize their thinking instead of clinging to the outdated structures that have slowed progress for decades.

This future is not inevitable. And the world has reached the point where choosing otherwise is no longer sustainable.

A future where women lead and participate fully is about correcting a structural imbalance that has limited global progress for generations. When women are included, systems stop wasting talent, time, and money. They stop designing solutions around partial data. They stop accepting inefficiency as inevitable. Inclusion isn't charity; it's operational excellence.

A world where women everywhere have access to innovations is a world where the economic trajectory of countries shifts permanently. Healthy women work. Healthy women innovate. Healthy women invest in their families and communities. Healthy women create stable societies. No other demographic investment has this level of consistent return.

The world changes when women aren't fighting preventable health issues every step of the way.

The most profound shift comes from reimagining aging. The future where women live longer and healthier rewrites the assumptions about who leads, who contributes, and who drives progress. Older women are already the backbone of communities everywhere. Healthy aging is a strategic metric.

> Inclusion isn't charity; it's operational excellence.

The future where women are healthy at every life stage is a future with a more stable workforce, higher innovation output, stronger families, and healthier populations. It's a future where gender-based health disparities no longer drain national budgets, and where women are not forced out of careers by preventable health issues. It's a future where girls grow up seeing women in leadership roles everywhere—in labs, hospitals, parliaments, and boardrooms—and understand that their own potential is unlimited.

This isn't about creating a world that's "better for women." It's about creating a world for everyone that finally performs at the level it's capable of.

And the truth is unavoidable: the countries, companies, and institutions that fully invest in women's health and leadership will define the next century. Progress has moved from philosophy to competition. The future is healthier, stronger, and more prosperous when women are fully included, and the places that embrace that will be the places that thrive.

If you zoom out and look at the future through the lens of global strategy—not politics, ideology, or tradition—the world becomes incredibly clear. The next era belongs to the societies that treat women's health as the economic engine it's always been. Growth accelerates. Institutions stabilize. Innovation compounds. Generations benefit.

Impact Requires Trust

The most compelling progress in women's health doesn't come from theoretical models. It comes from organizations operating under real constraints, turning limited resources into scalable solutions without lowering the standard of care. These groups have proven, repeatedly, that the barriers holding women back are solvable when you stop designing for idealized health systems and start designing for the world as it is.

One of the clearest examples is the rapid progress happening in cervical cancer screening and prevention. For years, cervical cancer was treated as an inevitable killer in many low- and middle-income countries. Screening rates remained low, follow-up systems failed, and cultural stigma around gynecological exams kept millions of women away. But the shift to self-collected HPV testing paired with digital follow-up tools is rewriting that narrative.

CureCervicalCancer (CCC) is reshaping preventative care by designing screening methods centered on dignity, comfort, and trauma sensitivity. HERhealthEQ has partnered with the organization to deploy cervical cancer treatment equipment in Vietnam. CCC's model addresses fear of pelvic exams, past trauma, mistrust in the system, discomfort with traditional screening environments, and logistical barriers to care.

By offering self-collection options and designing experiences around women's emotional and physical safety, CCC is removing one of the largest silent barriers in women's preventive care. It has deployed HPV self-collection screening programs across Africa, Latin America, and Asia, partnering with local clinics and health systems in countries such as Kenya, Guatemala, India, and Tanzania to expand access to early cervical cancer detection. Hundreds of thousands of women have been screened and thousands have been treated for precancerous lesions. This approach—meeting women where they are rather than forcing compliance via travel and antiquated systems not built for them—represents the future of screening globally.

We can eliminate cervical cancer with practical, evidence-based strategies that respect women's realities.

And because these interventions are so tightly connected to women's lived experiences, the organizations delivering them have become incredibly skilled at balancing technical rigor with cultural nuance. These organizations understand something global health has been slow to accept: impact requires trust. You cannot improve health outcomes at scale if women don't trust the system treating them.

When you build trust, women return for care. When women return, outcomes improve. It's that simple.

When organizations take cultural and emotional realities seriously, uptake skyrockets. The health system becomes something women interact with intentionally rather than reluctantly. And that shift changes everything: early detection improves, chronic conditions are managed earlier, and the long-term cost burden on the system decreases.

You cannot improve health outcomes at scale if women don't trust the system treating them.

What ties these global health success stories together is their realism. They build for constraints, not fantasies. They create systems that work with intermittent power, limited staff, high patient volumes, and cultural complexity. They understand that scaling is about fit, adoption, and trust.

Impact in women's health accelerates when solutions honor women's lived experiences rather than ignoring them.

The Money Shift

The progress we're seeing today is also powered by funding models that break the old dependency cycle. Major funders are shifting in ways that align with these ground-truth models. Alignment between philanthropy, social innovation, and local health systems is what accelerates real-world impact.

The rise of revenue-generating nonprofit models, blended finance strategies, pooled funds, and circular economies is freeing organizations from that treadmill of constant NGO fundraising. These models create financial resilience, allowing organizations to scale based on success, not donor whims.

Women's health investments are climbing—still insufficient but rising faster than ever before. It's smart economics. It's strategic investment. It's market creation.

What used to be undervalued is now unavoidable.

For years, the global conversation around women's health focused on what might be possible "one day." But that isn't where we are anymore. The last decade has shown us that when women are centered—not accommodated, not included as a checkbox—health systems change, economies shift, outcomes improve, and entirely new markets emerge.

Another of the most promising models emerging now is the public-interest startup, a structure that blends mission with market discipline. These startups design for affordability, maintain equity as a core metric, and build sustainability through financially viable products. The global health ecosystem has historically struggled to support models that are neither fully nonprofit nor fully commercial. But the women's health movement is changing that.

These transformations aren't emerging from massive institutions alone. Many of the biggest leaps are coming from mid-sized NGOs, hybrid social enterprises, startups inside LMICs, and cross-border collaborations that operate with urgency instead of bureaucracy. These organizations aren't theorizing. They're implementing under the harshest constraints imaginable and outperforming legacy institutions while they do it.

Remove the Silos

What's different now is that many organizations and their work are no longer siloed. Their stories are beginning to converge into a visible pattern: women's health outcomes improve fastest when solutions are designed with women, powered by local talent, and supported through sustainable financial models that don't collapse when the next crisis emerges.

This shift is accelerating because more people are stepping into the industry to reinvent past models.

ENDING DELAYS IN CARE THROUGH PROACTIVE COMMUNITY HEALTH

Muso, a company based in West Africa, has reimagined how community healthcare works. I first learned about its model while beginning projects in Ghana. What stood out immediately was its simplicity: instead of waiting for women to find the health system, the system goes to them.

In many communities, care technically exists but it's practically inaccessible. Distance, cost, transportation, and caregiving responsibilities delay treatment until illness becomes severe. By the time a patient reaches a clinic, a treatable condition may have become life-threatening.

Muso redesigned the model entirely.

Instead of relying on clinics as the first point of contact, trained community health workers visit households door-to-door, screening families for early signs of illness. They provide treatment for common conditions or connect patients to nearby clinics through rapid referral systems.

The approach is simple: find illness early, treat immediately, escalate quickly when needed.

The results have been striking. In Yirimadio, Mali, where Muso first piloted the model, under-five mortality fell by more than 90 percent between 2008 and 2015, one of the fastest documented reductions in sub-Saharan Africa.

The real innovation was design, not technology. Muso shifted the burden of access away from patients and onto the health system itself.

The organizations turning the tide understand the truth that global health was too slow to acknowledge; women's health outcomes are universally tied to delays—delays caused by distance, stigma, cost, misinformation, or distrust. Eliminate the delays, and mortality plummets.

But beyond last-mile care, other groups are tackling structural inequities at entirely different layers of the system.

Take diagnostic access. In many regions, the most dangerous part of a woman's health journey isn't childbirth or cancer. It's the gap between suspicion and diagnosis. When that gap stretches into months, women die. When it shrinks, they live.

CANCER TREATMENT ACCESS FOR WOMEN WITH NO PATHWAY TO CARE

I first learned about The Max Foundation through HERhealthEQ. To better inform the work we were planning, I was discussing cancer programs in LMICs with a colleague at Partners In Health, one of Max Foundation's collaborators. Its work addresses a common reality in global health: millions of women diagnosed with treatable cancers never receive treatment because there's no pathway to access it.

In many low-resource settings, cancer care breaks down at every step. Diagnostics are limited, medicines are unaffordable, and long-term treatment programs are rare and mainly concentrated around the large capital cities. Survival often depends less on the disease than on whether a patient can access therapy.

The Max Foundation approached the problem differently. Instead of waiting for full oncology systems to emerge, it built a partnership model that connects pharmaceutical companies, local hospitals, and patients.

The model focuses on three elements:

- Negotiating donated or deeply subsidized medicines from pharmaceutical companies
- Partnering with local hospitals to strengthen diagnostic and monitoring capacity
- Supporting adherence and supply continuity so patients can remain on long-term treatment

Rather than building new infrastructure, the model unlocks access within existing systems.

The results have been significant. Through partnerships with global pharmaceutical companies and treatment centers in more than eighty countries, the Max Foundation has enabled tens of thousands of patients to access lifesaving cancer therapies that would otherwise be unavailable.

Partnership-based access programs can dramatically expand treatment and reduce mortality, even where traditional health infrastructure is limited. Sometimes the fastest way to save lives is not building entirely new systems but connecting the ones that already exist.

The biggest gains in women's health come from ecosystems of innovation, not single solutions. Organizations working at different points along the care journey reinforce one another, and the whole system gets stronger because of it.

But innovation isn't limited to clinical care. Increasingly, financial inclusion is emerging as one of the most powerful health interventions.

When women control financial resources, they access care earlier, stay in treatment longer, and make health decisions without depending on gatekeepers. Some of the most creative organizations in the women's health movement are using economic tools, not medical ones, to unlock access.

ECONOMIC EMPOWERMENT AS A HEALTH INTERVENTION

While researching models that successfully expand women's access to care, one organization appears repeatedly: Bangladesh Rural Advancement Committee. Operating across South Asia and Africa, BRAC has built one of the largest development organizations in the world. It's also one of the clearest examples of how economic empowerment and health outcomes are deeply connected.

In many communities, women don't avoid healthcare because they lack awareness. They avoid it because they can't afford it. The cost of transportation, medications, or time away from work can make seeking care financially impossible.

BRAC reframed the problem: access to healthcare is often a financial barrier disguised as a medical one.

Instead of separating health programs from economic development, BRAC integrated them. The model combines microfinance and savings programs, community health workers, maternal health education, and women's livelihood support.

The impact has been measurable. Women participating in BRAC programs show higher rates of antenatal care attendance, contraceptive use, and overall health service utilization compared to women outside the programs.

Economic agency is a health intervention. When women have financial control and income stability, accessing healthcare becomes possible.

When you zoom out, these organizations—HERhealthEQ, CureCervicalCancer, Muso, the Max Foundation, BRAC, and many others—form a constellation of impact that's reshaping global women's health. They are the future of the sector. Collectively, they prove this movement is not waiting for permission.

Women's health innovation is no longer constrained to a narrow set of conditions. It spans maternal health, chronic disease, diagnostics, financial models, supply chains, mental health, and preventative care. Impact is happening in every direction at once because women's needs are interconnected.

It's important to understand that none of these breakthroughs required massive infrastructure overhauls. They required partnerships, creativity, humility, and a refusal to accept that women around the world should settle for less. The impact becomes undeniable when you look at how these organizations, each with a different model, fit together to fill the gaps the formal global health system has repeatedly failed to close.

This illustrates why newer, more adaptive funding models are so important. The old paradigm treated NGOs as project implementers, not as system builders. It forced them to shape their missions around donor cycles rather than around impact. The new paradigm—blended finance mechanisms, revenue-generating nonprofits, catalytic philanthropy, pooled corporate funds—is enabling women's health innovators to survive and scale.

The impact is magnified by the recognition that women's health is the cornerstone of national development. It is infrastructure, and it explains why investment is rising.

In the last twenty-five years, I've witnessed us move from never speaking about women's health to shouting it from the New York Stock Exchange closing bell. Even in the last five years, we've gone from FemTech being a new niche category to women's health beginning to flow into general healthcare categories and show real returns. To witness this change is astonishing, yet I know how much more work we need to do.

We are not waiting for a future where women's health becomes a priority. That future is already here.

What we're waiting to see is whether we scale it fast enough to meet the moment.

What's Possible

So the question becomes: what does that future look like when the systems have finally caught up?

It looks like governments where gender parity is normal, not celebrated. Women serve as ministers of finance, health, education, environment, and foreign affairs because they're qualified and it's normalized. Legislation reflects the needs of real families: childcare is available, parental leave is standard, mental health is protected, and freedom of choice is treated as a national security issue. In these governments, women influence budgets, policy agendas, and crisis response at the same rate as men. The result is steadier governance and stronger public trust.

It looks like healthcare systems where women lead hospitals, research institutions, professional associations, and regulatory bodies. You see funding directed toward early detection, chronic disease management, reproductive health, mental health, and aging—all areas that cut massive costs when handled proactively. You see clinical training grounded in modern science instead of outdated gender assumptions. You see workforce policies built around sustainability rather than martyrdom. And you see systems that finally function as designed because leadership reflects the workforce and the population.

It looks like innovation pipelines where women shape the problems worth solving. You get drug discovery that recognizes sex-based biology from day one, not as an afterthought. You get AI systems that diagnose women accurately because the data reflects reality. You get devices designed for diverse anatomy, not for a single default user. You get digital health tools that account for safety, privacy, and ease of use but because women helped build them.

It looks like investment firms with women's health as part of their general healthcare thesis. You see significant capital being allocated to funding women's health innovations in early stages as well as the growth, commercialization, and scale phases. You have capital invested in health conditions that are currently considered niche because the investment case has been made. You get innovations that cater to all women, in all geographies, with equal access to capital as men. You have investment fund-of-funds that support the finance managers who continue to fund women's health at scale on a global level.

It looks like younger women and girls growing up in a world where opportunity is not conditional on luck, geography, or whether they can navigate systems built against them. Girls are educated without interruption. They enter a workforce that expects them, not tolerates them. They pursue STEM, business, policy, medicine, and leadership roles because they've seen women excel in all those areas.

It looks like global health initiatives that prioritize local expertise and women-led organizations. Funding doesn't trickle down through layers of bureaucracy before reaching the people who need it. Instead, local innovators—women who understand the cultural and practical realities of their communities—direct resources where they will have the most impact. This shift alone transforms outcomes across Africa, Asia, Latin America, and the Middle East.

It looks like all women finally receiving the care they deserve, not simply for the sake of procreation. Hot flashes aren't dismissed as exaggeration. Osteoporosis screening is standard. Cardiovascular disease is caught early. Cancer detection is routine. Cognitive decline is addressed proactively. Women in their fifties, sixties, and beyond stay in leadership roles because their health supports longevity. And societies benefit enormously from the continued participation of the most experienced demographic in the workforce.

> When you invest in women, the world gets better. Always.

That's the future that becomes possible when women's health is treated as infrastructure, foundational, and essential to societal function.

But to get there, individual action, institutional action, and collective action all matter. Women can't do this alone. Men can't sit on the sidelines. Institutions can't wait for "the right moment." Governments can't assume progress is self-perpetuating. Everyone has a role.

The future isn't guaranteed. It's chosen and designed. And for the first time, we have enough data, examples, momentum, leadership, and global awareness to choose better. The gains are immediate and generational. A world where women are healthy and included at every level lifts entire societies.

If there is one truth this book should leave ringing in your mind, it's this: when you invest in women, the world gets better. Always.

That is the future worth building. And it starts today.

Chapter 9 Takeaways

- **THE FUTURE OF WOMEN'S HEALTH IS ALREADY BEING BUILT.** THE ORGANIZATIONS, LEADERS, AND FUNDING MODELS PROVING WHAT WORKS TODAY ARE DEFINING THE NEXT ERA OF HEALTH AND ECONOMIC GROWTH.
- **COUNTRIES THAT INVEST IN WOMEN WILL OUTPERFORM THOSE THAT DO NOT.** WOMEN'S HEALTH, EDUCATION, AND LEADERSHIP DRIVE STRONGER ECONOMIES, MORE STABLE INSTITUTIONS, AND GREATER LONG-TERM RESILIENCE.
- **THE NEXT BREAKTHROUGHS WILL COME FROM SOLUTIONS BUILT FOR TRUST, ACCESS, AND REAL-WORLD CONDITIONS.** THE WINNERS WILL BE MODELS THAT MEET WOMEN WHERE THEY ARE AND TURN CONSTRAINTS INTO SCALABLE DESIGN.
- **WOMEN'S HEALTH IS A COMPETITIVE ADVANTAGE AND A DEVELOPMENT IMPERATIVE.** THE FUTURE BELONGS TO THE INSTITUTIONS AND SOCIETIES THAT TREAT WOMEN'S HEALTH AS INFRASTRUCTURE AND SCALE WHAT ALREADY WORKS.

Chapter 10: Call to Arms

The truth is simple: no single person is big enough to carry a movement that serves half the world. Not me, not you, not any one organization or government. The scale of women's health, its impact, its urgency, and its potential is far bigger than the loudest voices or the most visible leaders. That's the point. Movements thrive because they outgrow their founders. They gain momentum because more hands join the work. They endure because they refuse to stay small.

Women's health has reached that tipping point.

That's why this movement can't be a trend, a marketing cycle, or a "moment." It can't depend on headlines or election years.

As Liz Powell, president of G2G Consulting and founder of the Women's Health Advocates, said bluntly and correctly at a gathering of women's health leaders: "Women's health is not having a moment. It's a movement."

Movements don't evaporate when the attention moves elsewhere. They persist because the need is real, the data is overwhelming, and the momentum is finally compounding instead of dissipating.

What's happening right now is unprecedented. In the last few years, women's health has gained a level of visibility that was unthinkable even a decade ago. It's not perfect, it's not comprehensive, and it's certainly not enough. But it's real. New funding pools exist that didn't before. Research agendas are shifting. Governments are finally acknowledging gendered health inequities in policy. Organizations are forming networks that didn't exist five years ago. And women inside institutions who are finally reaching seats where decisions are made are refusing to be the only ones in the room.

We are the ecosystem that must carry the movement forward. Not any one sector, not any one political ideology, not any one region. It's a coalition by necessity. Government, private sector, nonprofits, philanthropy, academia, investors, clinicians, innovators, and advocates all have jobs to do. If they do them in silos, nothing will change. If they do them together, the movement becomes unstoppable.

Collaboration

People love to say "collaboration is important," but here's the real reason it matters: no single domain holds all the levers. Policy alone won't fix research bias. Funding alone won't fix access. Innovation alone won't fix workforce inequity. Advocacy alone won't fix entrenched systems. The wins that have mattered over the past few years have happened because cross-sector collaboration forced something open.

Take the White House Women's Health Research Initiative, launched by First Lady Dr. Jill Biden in 2023. I was part of that initiative, and what struck me was how deliberately broad the work had to be. Policy leads, federal agencies, researchers, patient advocates, economists, clinicians, and innovators collaborated because the solution was a systemic reboot. You don't get that kind of momentum without multiple sectors rowing in the same direction.

Or look at the Africa NCD Alliance, of which I'm a member. It puts government, private industry, academics, nonprofits, and investors in the same room because the gaps in women's health are too big and too expensive for any one group to solve alone. These aren't networking clubs. They're pressure systems. When you bring people with capital, data, influence, and lived experience together, you accelerate change.

And then there are organizations like the Women's Health PAC in the US, Women in Global Health, and other emerging advocacy engines that are shaping political will, directing funding, and elevating women who are running for office or leading healthcare systems. None of these existed at this scale a decade ago. That's how you know this is infrastructure.

Policy is shifting too, and not in tiny symbolic ways. We're seeing real wins:

- Expanded coverage for postpartum care in the US and many European countries
- Rwanda's national digital health ID

- Australia's cervical cancer elimination timeline and international commitments to cervical cancer elimination
- US insurance reforms that address breast density notifications and additional screening leading to expanded European and Asian notifications
- Early investments in menopause research and workforce protections.
- The EU's clinical trial regulation updates requiring sex-disaggregated data
- The WHO's expanded HPV vaccination globally

These gains didn't happen because one person fought hard enough. They happened because networks of people pushed, pressured, educated, organized, and refused to back down. Collaboration is the engine.

But here's the uncomfortable truth: a movement this big can't rely on leadership alone. It needs succession. It needs mentorship. It needs people willing to step aside, step up, or step in depending on what the moment requires. Legacy is about whether the work continues once you're gone.

If you want to make a dent:

- **Join the existing collectives.** Women's Health Innovation Network, global alliances, cross-border business exchanges, and professional communities exist to accelerate impact.
- **Connect with innovators and executives.** They need allies, advocates, and amplifiers.
- **Work with institutions and companies, even the slow ones.** Change is hardest there, but the returns are enormous.
- **Bring men into the work.** They're part of the problem when we exclude them from the solution.

Your individual action matters. But multiplied by others, it becomes movement. And once a movement gains momentum, it becomes impossible to stop.

Change Is Happening Everywhere

One of the most significant shifts occurring right now is the way leadership pathways in women's health are being rebuilt—not tweaked, rebuilt—to ensure this movement has staying power. When women lead, priorities finally match reality.

Look at the leadership changes happening across healthcare. We now have women running major health systems, global health organizations, biotech companies, public health agencies, investor networks, and federal initiatives. It's not nearly enough, but it's more than ever before. This matters because women leaders are far more likely to prioritize issues that have historically been considered "niche" or "secondary". But it took women reaching decision-making roles to get them recognized as such.

The truth is that women's leadership is itself an intervention.

One woman in leadership forces a door open. Ten women keep it open. A thousand women redesign the building.

You can see this ripple effect on the policy changes that have already happened. Maternal mortality review committees now exist in nearly all US states because women leaders insisted on it. The World Health Organization issued global self-care guidelines allowing women to access certain health services outside traditional clinical settings, including self-administered contraception, self-testing for STIs like HIV, and HPV self-collection for cervical cancer screening. Postpartum Medicaid coverage has been extended in dozens of states because women in statehouses refused to accept a sixty-day cutoff as "good enough." These and many other notification laws and screening reforms—changes that are literally saving women's lives—came from advocates, researchers, and policymakers working together for years.

The same kind of leadership shift is showing up globally. Countries are adopting gender-inclusive health policies, expanding access to HPV vaccination, and investing in cervical cancer elimination because women in ministries of health, research councils, and civil society pushed these issues out of the margins. These are the kinds of changes that accumulate quietly until suddenly they're impossible to ignore.

These efforts are coordinated, they're growing, and they're not relying on traditional hierarchies. That's what a movement does. It applies sustained pressure in multiple places at once.

Work isn't only happening at the top. It's happening at the grassroots, in professional networks, in community health centers, inside hospital systems, on social platforms, and at kitchen tables. The most effective change often comes from people who never had influence in the past: nurses pushing for workforce protections, community health workers advocating for resources, midwives expanding access to care, patient advocates reshaping clinical trial recruitment, and innovators building technologies they needed but couldn't find.

One woman in leadership forces a door open. Ten women keep it open. A thousand women redesign the building.

Movements are loud on the outside but quiet on the inside. The headlines show the wins, but the work happens in small rooms, in late nights, in conversations that aren't recorded, and in decisions that don't get public praise. It happens when someone speaks up in a meeting they weren't invited to but attended anyway. When a woman challenges a budget that excludes women's health priorities. When a leader hires a woman who has never been given a fair shot. When someone refuses to let a biased research protocol move forward. When a group of women call out a policy gap and refuse to let it drop.

The movement has also been fueled by women founders, executives, and innovators who were dismissed for years until their ideas and companies proved the cynics wrong. They saw needs no one else saw, built products no one else would build, and pushed into markets most investors ignored. These women were catalysts.

Real change happens in accumulated daily choices made by thousands of people who are aligned around the same mission: women deserve healthcare that is designed for them, governed by them, informed by them, and led by them.

And yet, for all the progress, there's still a gap between the size of the problem and the scale of our response. Because a movement this large will only go as far as the people who choose to join it.

Entry Points

Participation is the final ingredient that will determine whether this movement becomes permanent. The measure of a movement is enrollment, not enthusiasm. And enrollment requires clarity on how people, especially you, can plug in without wondering if your efforts matter.

Because they do. Every single one does.

The temptation in any large movement is to assume the "real work" is happening somewhere else—inside governments, think tanks, big companies, hospitals, and networks with funding and influence. But that assumption lets too many people off the hook. Movements grow because regular people decide they're part of it. They grow because someone chooses to act on a Tuesday afternoon when no one is watching. They grow because someone refuses to let a harmful status quo go unchallenged. They grow because someone realizes their sphere of influence—no matter how small it seems—is larger than they thought.

So, the natural question becomes: how do you meaningfully contribute to a movement that's already in motion?

You start where you are, both physically and geographically.

If you work in healthcare, you can push for representation on boards and committees, in leadership pipelines, clinical teams, R&D, procurement decisions, trial recruitment, meetings, and workforce policies. You can question practices that assume men are the default patient. You can advocate for data disaggregation. You can challenge decisions made without women at the table. You can fund a new product focused on women's health. You can push for shifts in compensation, promotion, and staffing that reflect who's actually doing the work. Your job description may not say "fix gender inequity," but you're surrounded by opportunities to do exactly that.

If you work in innovation or tech, build with women from day one. Ensure women are in the room when product decisions are made. Don't wait until late-stage development to discover your design doesn't fit women's anatomy, physiology, safety needs, schedules, or financial constraints. Make inclusive design the default. Solve problems that matter. Build for the women who aren't being served including in emerging markets. And don't fall into the trap of calling every women-centered solution "niche." Nothing about serving half the population is niche.

If you're in investment, funding, corporate strategy, or philanthropy, you have leverage others don't. Direct capital toward women-led companies and women-focused innovations. Push for women's health to be included in healthcare verticals, not carved off into the "miscellaneous" bucket. Ask better questions: where are the gaps? What hasn't been funded? Whose ideas are being ignored? Whose solutions are being deprioritized because they aren't led by traditional innovators? Why isn't our company investing in women's health? Where are our investments in women's health? The market is clear: women's health delivers outsized returns. The missed opportunity is staggering. You can change that.

If you're a policymaker, regulator, legislative staffer, or advocate, you already know how much policy shapes women's health. Keep pushing. Push for reimbursement parity. Push for postpartum coverage expansion, maternal mental health integration, cervical cancer elimination strategies, menopause research funding, and better workforce policies for the overwhelmingly female care workforce. Push for data transparency. Push for accountability. But also, create the mechanisms for women to testify, advise, and lead. Policy changes when women are the beneficiaries and the architects.

If you work in education, research, or public health, you have the power to shape narratives and knowledge. Teach women's health as a core requirement, not an elective. Build curricula that include sex-based biology, physiology, and pharmacology. Ensure students understand how disparities are created and how to dismantle them. Don't let the next generation inherit the blind spots of the past.

If you're a leader at any level, your influence is larger than you think. If you hire, promote, budget, schedule, evaluate, or design systems, you're shaping the conditions under which women work and thrive. Advocate for equitable parental leave, flexible scheduling, safer workplaces, mentorship pathways, and advancement opportunities. Allocate P&L to women's health initiatives. Normalize women's health needs in the workplace. Hire women. Lead like the future depends on it, because it does.

And if you're outside all these sectors, if you're "just one person," you're still needed. Movements need voters, consumers, patients, community members, mentors, donors, amplifiers, and advocates. They need people who ask better questions in exam rooms. They need people who demand better coverage from insurers. They need people who refuse to let harmful comments slide into workplaces or social circles. They need people who talk openly about women's health, so stigma loses its power. They need people who show up.

There are millions of small entry points into this movement, and every single one expands its reach.

Because ultimately, this movement is not about any one initiative, organization, company, institution, or leader. It's about shifting the global trajectory of health, power, and opportunity. It's about refusing to tolerate systems that were never built for women and choosing to build new ones.

What makes this movement powerful is that it's grounded in measurable reality. The evidence backs us. The outcomes validate us. The economics support us. The momentum is accelerating. The policy landscape is shifting. The innovation ecosystem is expanding. The investment climate is waking up. The workforce is demanding change. The global health community is paying attention. This isn't a moment that will fade because it was never a moment. It was a course-correction centuries in the making.

We aren't waiting for permission anymore. We're building, pushing, reshaping, and rebalancing. It's about distributed power, shared ownership, and a collective uprising made of data, outcomes, economics, advocacy, innovation, and lived experience.

The next chapter of this movement will be written by the people who decide they're part of it.

And here's the final truth: the movement is bigger than you, but it needs you.

It needs your voice, your courage, your skills, your influence, your networks, your advocacy, your mentorship, your willingness to challenge the old and build the new.

Be the Change

Meaningful change requires transfer of power. When women move into leadership roles and then immediately reach back to pull others with them, the system changes for good. This movement will live or die by an abundance mindset. There is space for more women, there is power to share, and there is enough credit to go around.

But the movement can't rely solely on women lifting women. Men have an essential role. Men hold a majority of the senior leadership positions across healthcare, academia, policy, and investment. Men who use their power to open doors instead of guard them amplify the movement dramatically. Some of the fastest reforms in institutions have happened because male leaders acknowledged the inequities and actively cleared space for women to lead. Not as a gesture, but as a strategic decision.

When you have women across industries, across age groups, and across political lines pushing for the same outcomes, everyone wins.

There's also a growing recognition that the innovations we need won't come from any one region. Women's health is global, and some of the most effective solutions have been born outside the traditional power centers. These innovations are blueprints, not "emerging market pilots." The movement grows stronger every time the center of gravity expands.

Cross-sectional pressure is one of the most powerful signs that the movement is maturing. When you have women across industries, across age groups, and across political lines pushing for the same outcomes, everyone wins.

Your One Thing

There's always a turning point in any movement when the truth becomes too obvious to ignore. We're standing in that moment right now. Women's health is a global economic engine sitting idle because the world keeps pretending the cost of inaction is tolerable. It isn't. And if you've read this, you already feel the pull of that reality.

We've spent decades underinvesting in half the population and then acting surprised when the economy underperforms and health systems buckle. The numbers don't lie: inequity drains trillions, derails careers, stunts innovation, and destabilizes families and countries. But the returns when women's health is prioritized are immediate, measurable, and transformational. Every barrier removed unlocks an entire chain of economic and social benefits. Every woman who stays healthier, lives longer, and thrives professionally strengthens her family and her community. It's documented, repeatable, and scalable.

But facts alone don't change systems. People do. And most people, even well-intentioned ones, wait for someone else to go first.

I didn't know what I was doing when I began this work. I didn't have a strategic roadmap, a long-term plan, or a team of experts telling me I'd succeed. I had discomfort, frustration, and a sense that the world wasn't working the way it should. That's it. And that's all most people ever start with. Movements are rarely built from certainty. They're built from irritation, instinct, and a willingness to act before everything makes sense.

You don't need readiness. You need motion.

> You don't have to reinvent the wheel, but the wheel won't turn unless you push it.

If you're waiting to feel qualified before stepping in, stop. No one in women's health, global health, policy, or innovation arrived "ready." They arrived willing. They learned on the way down, on the way up, or somewhere in the turbulence of building something faster than the world understood it.

Everyone gets it wrong at some point. Everyone learns by doing.

Every innovator, every advocate, every builder started out uncertain. As Nelson Mandela said, "Courage was not the absence of fear, but the triumph over it."

If you're afraid, good. That means you're standing in a place where the outcome matters. The goal is impact, not perfection. Start here:

- **Choose your lane of influence.** Pick the area where you can move the fastest with the least friction.
- **Pick one problem that keeps you awake and move toward it.** Big or small, the size doesn't matter. Focus does.
- **Stop waiting for permission to lead.** No one's going to hand it to you.
- **Do the next right thing.** Make the call. Send the email. Approve the budget. Write the policy line. Introduce the executive. Raise your hand. Name the bias. Ask the uncomfortable question. Fund the pilot. Challenge an assumption. Increase representation.
- **Repeat.** Momentum is built one decision at a time.
- **Bring others with you.** Movements scale because people talk, share, invite, and amplify.

Don't think of these as small steps. Think of them as accelerators. They're how systems change—not through grand gestures, but through relentless, compounding action.

You don't have to reinvent the wheel, but the wheel won't turn unless you push it.

The question I hear most often is, "Where do I even start?" The truth is, you already have. Reading this book means you've crossed a threshold most people never reach: the point where the status quo becomes intolerable. The rest is execution, which begins with one intentional choice.

Women's health isn't a monolith. It's a universe of problems that require different skill sets, different levels of influence, and different kinds of thinkers. There's room for you regardless of your title, industry, gender, location, or background. You don't need to be a clinician to change clinical outcomes. You don't need to be a policymaker to shift policy. You don't need to be an investor to influence how capital flows.

You just need to decide that this matters enough to act.

While women's health needs big, structural change, it also needs the unglamorous, immediate fixes that compound faster than people realize.

If you do even one of these, the trajectory changes. That's the point. Trajectories shift long before systems do.

Which brings us to your moment of choice. Not dramatic. Not cinematic. Just real.

Ask yourself one question: *What is the one action I will commit to right now that will move women's health forward?*

When you commit to just one action, you signal to the world that you are part of this shift. You are part of the reason inequities won't be able to hide behind bureaucracy or outdated norms anymore. You are someone who doesn't wait for permission to build what should have existed all along.

Chapter 10 Takeaways

- **WOMEN'S HEALTH IS NO LONGER A MOMENT; IT'S A MOVEMENT.** ITS NEXT PHASE WILL BE DRIVEN BY COORDINATED ACTION ACROSS INSTITUTIONS, INDUSTRIES, AND COMMUNITIES.
- **CROSS-SECTOR COLLABORATION IS HOW SYSTEMS CHANGE AT SCALE.** POLICY, CAPITAL, RESEARCH, INNOVATION, AND ADVOCACY MUST MOVE TOGETHER OR THE SYSTEM WILL KEEP REPRODUCING THE SAME FAILURES.
- **THIS MOVEMENT GROWS WHEN MORE PEOPLE DECIDE TO PARTICIPATE, NOT JUST OBSERVE.** REAL PROGRESS COMES FROM DAILY ACTS OF PRESSURE, LEADERSHIP, MENTORSHIP, INVESTMENT, AND ACCOUNTABILITY ACROSS EVERY LEVEL OF INFLUENCE.
- **THE CALL TO ACTION IS SIMPLE: PICK ONE LANE, TAKE ONE STEP, AND KEEP MOVING** SYSTEMS DO NOT CHANGE BECAUSE PEOPLE FEEL READY. THEY CHANGE BECAUSE PEOPLE ACT BEFORE PERMISSION ARRIVES.

AUTHOR'S NOTE

I never set out to write a book. I started writing articles for myself, trying to organize what has been living in scattered pieces in my brain for years. Decades of work in women's health around the world, thousands of conversations with clinicians, investors, founders, and patients, and a growing frustration I couldn't shake. The articles got longer, and before I knew it, I was writing a book. Something I never imagined I'd do.

What drove me was anger. Anger at how many smart, credentialed people could diagnose what was broken in women's health and then stop there. State the facts. Publish the data. Express concern. But never come up with a solution. I wanted to explore what we can do together to make a change and build the solid foundation that should have been built years ago. I want us to get to a place where we can stop talking about it because it's been solved and we're building the rest of the infrastructure around us.

I'll be honest: this is terrifying. There are others who are just as qualified as I am to write this book. Probably more qualified. I'm not a physician. I'm not a policymaker. I'm not an academic researcher. I'm a CEO, an investor, and an operator who's spent twenty-five years inside the system, and I can see what's broken and what's possible. That perspective matters and putting it into the world like this means giving up my privacy. It means opening myself up to critique from those who disagree with my framing, my conclusions, and my right to have this conversation.

But I'm doing it anyway. I'm willing to take the risk if it means making life better for women around the world. I can't sit still and be quiet any longer. I need to speak out in the hope that others, or even just one, will do something to change this world.

I'm choosing to play big. Here's what that looks like in practice:

I'm speaking to get this message out. Locally and globally, in front of small and large rooms. In cosmopolitan areas, in regional locations, and in communities everywhere. Wherever the conversation needs to be had, I'm going to show up and have it.

I'm investing in women's health around the world. Through personal capital, funds, blended finance structures, and direct investments. Participating in venture capital, advising companies, and saying yes to opportunities that put resources behind the people doing the work.

I'm advocating for better women's health in local, regional, national, and global spaces. Sometimes it's legislative advocacy. Sometimes it's pushing the global standards for how women access care and information. Sometimes it's educating women from a business perspective so they can walk into rooms and demand better.

I'm growing companies. DeepLook Medical, HERhealthEQ, the companies I sit on the boards of, the ones I advise, and the ones that haven't been built yet. When women's health companies grow, the entire industry gains visibility and better information. When projects like HERhealthEQ's expand, women in underserved areas get access to better quality medical care designed specifically for them. When the companies I lead or advise succeed, it means better returns, better implementation at scale, better diagnostics and care, and more returns in capital and investment.

I wish this wasn't an issue that needed solving, but it is and I had to do something. But I can't do it alone and need everyone alongside me and the others doing the work.

So I'll ask you again, and more directly this time: What is your one action?

Not the one you think you should take. Not the one that sounds impressive. Not the one you might get to "after things slow down."

The one you can do today.

Write it down. Say it out loud. Share it with someone you trust.

Movements don't grow through intentions. They grow through declarations.

And they succeed when enough people leap, even when the bridge isn't fully built.

We are building a future where women's health is prioritized, funded, researched, innovated, and protected. A future where policies reflect reality, where leadership reflects humanity, where healthcare reflects every body. A future where girls grow up knowing their health is not negotiable. A future where women age without being dismissed. A future where equity is engineered, not imagined. A future where the world finally runs on the full power of half its population.

That future is possible. That future is needed. That future is here. That future is waiting on you.

Leap anyway.

ACKNOWLEDGMENTS

Many people challenged my thinking, sharpened my arguments, and refused to let me get comfortable. This book is the result of their pressure, not my effort alone.

First, to those who directly shaped this manuscript, most especially the Lúcida team, your rigor made it better. To my editors, Cici and Katelin, thank you for pushing clarity over complexity and insisting that every claim earn its place. To the creative and technical team, Alma, Elisa, and Alexis, your creativity and expertise made this a reality. To the LOUD Management team, especially Amy and Liv, who continue to push me into bigger audiences where this work can take hold. To the people featured in the book who gave honest, unfiltered insight, your candor strengthened both the content and the conviction behind it.

To the colleagues, partners, and operators I've worked alongside over the last twenty-five years, this book is built on what I've learned with you in the field, not in theory. Every single interaction moved me and this topic forward. From my first international work in Costa Rica to the operators and clinics in Latin America and Africa, you continue to open my eyes to the reality of global healthcare. You've navigated the gaps, the trade-offs, and the realities of building in systems that were not designed to prioritize women. Your work is the proof behind every argument made here.

To the HERhealthEQ team and board members, current and past, without you much of the global impact work wouldn't be possible. Your trust in my vision, mission, and conviction allows us to directly improve women's global health. My hope for the next ten years is that we put ourselves out of business because our work is no longer needed.

To the leaders and advocates advancing women's health—especially those doing the work without recognition or resources—this book reflects your persistence. You've shown that progress doesn't come from moments. It comes from sustained pressure, disciplined execution, and refusal to accept the status quo.

To the women and men in the industry who have my back with support, understanding, and a sounding-board, thank you for your candor. To the broader women's health and healthcare community working to move policy and infrastructure forward, your work demonstrates what aligned, focused effort can actually achieve. It's a privilege to be part of that momentum.

To the women around the world putting everyone first before themselves, I hope this helps to build the infrastructure you need to start prioritizing your own health and prosperity. Every time I see you at a clinic focusing on your health, it lights me up inside. To the men who support her in healthcare and life, thank you for understanding how important she is to your life and to our society.

On a personal level, to my parents, your decades of support for my dreams, my convictions, and every audacious goal is what made this possible. I know my privilege to have been raised in your egalitarian household with the gift of choice. To my close friends and family, thank you for the support that made this possible—the time, patience, and understanding when this work demanded more than it should have, and for always being my cheerleaders.

And finally, to the women whose experiences continue to be overlooked, delayed, or dismissed, this book exists because the system hasn't earned the benefit of time. Awareness was never the goal. Change is.

This work isn't finished. It's being built.

GLOSSARY

AI: Artificial Intelligence: Computer systems designed to perform tasks that typically require human intelligence, such as learning, problem-solving, and pattern recognition.

Bikini medicine: A pejorative term for the historical reduction of women's health to only the body parts covered by a bikini, namely breasts and reproductive organs. The framing has narrowed research, funding, and clinical attention to fertility and gynecology while ignoring sex-specific differences in cardiovascular, neurological, autoimmune, and metabolic conditions.

Blended finance: The use of catalytic capital from public or philanthropic sources to increase private sector investment

Bangladesh Rural Advancement Committee (BRAC): One of the world's largest development organizations, working across South Asia and Africa in health, education, and economic empowerment

Burden of disease: The public health measure that quantifies the total impact of disease on a population, accounting for mortality, morbidity, and years lived with disability. The Global Burden of Disease study, referenced throughout this book, is the most widely used framework for this measurement.

Catalytic capital: Capital that accepts higher risk or lower returns in order to unlock additional private investment in high-impact but underserved markets. It's often deployed by foundations, development finance institutions, or impact investors to de-risk early-stage innovation.

Catalytic philanthropy: Philanthropic giving designed to spark systemic change by funding policy work, early-stage innovation, and ecosystem infrastructure, rather than direct services alone. It's structured to attract commercial follow-on investment once the market is proven.

CureCervicalCancer (CCC): A nonprofit organization redesigning cervical cancer screening around dignity, comfort, and trauma sensitivity

Circular economy of care: Model that captures and redirects functional medical equipment otherwise discarded through high-income country replacement cycles, refurbishing it for use in hospitals and clinics in low- and middle-income countries. It's the operating model behind HERhealthEQ.

Consumer Packaged Goods (CPG): Products that are sold quickly and at relatively low cost, such as food, beverages, toiletries, and other consumables

CSR: Corporate Social Responsibility: A business model where companies integrate social, environmental, and ethical concerns into their operations

Cardiovascular Disease (CVD): A group of conditions affecting the heart and blood vessels, the leading cause of death for women worldwide

DEI: Diversity, Equity, and Inclusion: Organizational frameworks and practices designed to promote fair treatment, equal opportunities, and full participation of all people, particularly those who have been historically marginalized or underrepresented

Dense breast tissue: Breast tissue composed of more fibrous and glandular tissue than fatty tissue, appearing white on mammograms in the same way tumors do. It affects roughly half of women globally, reduces mammography sensitivity, and is an independent risk factor for breast cancer.

Direct-to-Consumer (DTC): A business model where products are sold directly to customers without third-party intermediaries like wholesalers, retailers, or marketplaces

Earnings per share: Measures a company's profitability by determining how much a shareholder would receive per share owned if profits were distributed. It's calculated by subtracting preferred dividends from the company's net income, and then divided by the number of outstanding shares.

Employee resource group: Voluntary, employee-led groups formed around shared identities, backgrounds, or interests that foster a diverse, inclusive workplace, provide support, and help shape workplace priorities

Endometriosis: Chronic condition in which tissue similar to the uterine lining grows outside the uterus, causing pain, irregular bleeding, and infertility. It affects an estimated 190 million women globally and remains underdiagnosed, with diagnostic delays averaging seven to ten years.

Environmental, Social, and Governance (ESG): Criteria investors, consumers, and regulators use to evaluate a company's business practices and sustainability

Food and Drug Administration (FDA): U.S. federal agency responsible for protecting public health by regulating food, drugs, cosmetics, and medical devices

FemTech (Female Technology): Digital health tools, products, and services focused on women's well-being and health needs across the lifespan. First coined by FemTech entrepreneur Ida Tin.

Gross Domestic Product (GDP): The total monetary value of all goods and services produced within a country's borders

Gender-lens investing: An investment approach that considers gender-based factors in financial decision-making with the aim of closing gender gaps

Global Innovation Fund (GIF): A nonprofit blended finance vehicle that funds solutions delivering measurable social returns alongside market sustainability, using grants, loans, and equity in tranches

Global South: Regions of Latin America, Asia, Africa, and the Caribbean that are characterized by lower economic development, often used to describe low- and middle-income countries collectively

High-Income Country (HIC): Nations with high levels of economic development and per capita income, including but not limited to the US, Canada, Japan, Australia, the UK, and Switzerland

HIV (Human Immunodeficiency Virus): A virus that attacks the immune system, it's transmitted through blood and bodily fluids. Without treatment, it can progress to AIDS.

HPV (Human Papillomavirus): The most commonly sexually transmitted infection, it's a virus that can cause cervical cancer. It's preventable through vaccination.

IOF: International Osteoporosis Foundation, a global organization dedicated to the prevention, diagnosis, and treatment of osteoporosis

IP: Intellectual Property refers to the creations of the mind, such as inventions, designs, and artistic works, protected by law

Low-income countries (LICs): Nations with lower levels of economic development, including by not limited to Sudan, Uganda, Rwanda, and Afganistan

Low- and middle-income countries (LMIC): Nations with lower levels of economic development and per capita income, including but not limited to India, the Philippines, Mexico, Kenya, and Egypt

M-TIBA: Kenya-based mobile health wallet that allows users to save, send, and spend funds restricted to healthcare. Enables payers, providers, and patients to transact and track care delivery digitally, expanding access in regions with limited banking infrastructure.

Middle-income countries (MIC): Nations with moderate levels of economic development, including but not limited to India, Egypt, the Philippines, Kenya, Brazil, Mexico, and South Africa

Non-communicable disease (NCD): Chronic diseases not passed from person to person, such as heart disease, cancer, and diabetes

NGO: Non-governmental organization, a nonprofit group that operates independently of any government to address issues in support of public good

National Institutes of Health (NIH): US federal agency responsible for biomedical and public health research

OKR: Objectives and Key Results is a goal-setting framework used by organizations to define and track quarterly, biannual, and annual goals

Osteoporosis: Bone disease that develops when bone mineral density and mass decrease, weakening bones and increasing fracture risk. It disproportionately affects postmenopausal women due to estrogen loss.

PAC: Political Action Committee, an organization that raises money to elect or defeat political candidates

Public-private partnership: Cooperative arrangement between government and private sector entities to finance, build, and operate public infrastructure and services

R&D: Research and Development, or work directed toward innovation, introduction, and improvement of products and processes

Return on Investment (ROI): A measure used to evaluate the profitability and efficiency of an investment

Technical Advisory Group (TAG): Expert committees that provide specialized advice, recommendations, and guidance on complex technical, specific, scientific, or policy issues

TAM: Total Addressable Market, aka the maximum total revenue a company could generate if it captured the entire market demand for a specific product or service

Task shifting: Delegation of healthcare tasks from higher- to lower-skilled health workers

UN: United Nations, an international organization founded in 1945 to maintain global peace, security, and cooperation among nations

UNFPA: United Nations Population Fund, the UN organization focused on reproductive health and population issues

Women's Health Advocates (WHA): An organization focused on policy advocacy for women's health issues

WHO: World Health Organization, the UN agency responsible for international public health and safety

Women's health: Healthcare focused on diseases, conditions, and wellness needs specific to or disproportionately affecting women across their entire lifespan, beyond reproductive health alone

Women's health gap: Disparity between men's and women's health outcomes across diagnosis, treatment, research, and access. The McKinsey Health Institute estimates that closing this gap represents a trillion-dollar annual economic opportunity globally.

BIBLIOGRAPHY

Adamson, Adewole S., and Avery Smith. "Machine Learning and Health Care Disparities in Dermatology." *JAMA Dermatology* 154, no. 11 (2018): 1247–1248. https://doi.org/10.1001/jamadermatol.2018.2348.

Addati, Laura, Umberto Cattaneo, Valeria Esquivel, and Isabel Valarino. Care Work and Care Jobs for the Future of Decent Work. Geneva: International Labour Organization, 2018. https://www.ilo.org/publications/major-publications/care-work-and-care-jobs-future-decent-work.

Allemani, Claudia, et al. "Global Surveillance of Trends in Cancer Survival 2000–14 (CONCORD-3): Analysis of Individual Records for 37,513,025 Patients Diagnosed With One of 18 Cancers From 322 Population-Based Registries in 71 Countries." *The Lancet* 391, no. 10125 (2018): 1023–1075. https://doi.org/10.1016/S0140-6736(17)33326-3.

Allied Market Research. Femtech Market: Global Opportunity Analysis and Industry Forecast, 2024–2033. Portland, OR: Allied Market Research, 2024. https://www.alliedmarketresearch.com/femtech-market.

American Cancer Society. *Breast Cancer Facts & Figures 2023–2024*. Atlanta: American Cancer Society, 2023. https://www.cancer.org/research/cancer-facts-statistics/breast-cancer-facts-figures.html.

American Heart Association. "Heart Disease and Stroke Statistics—2023 Update: A Report From the American Heart Association." *Circulation* 147, no. 8 (2023). https://doi.org/10.1161/CIR.0000000000001123.

American Heart Association Ventures. https://www.heart.org/en/aha-ventures.

AOA Dx. *Follow the Exits: Why Women's Health is a Smart Bet in Healthcare.* AOA Diagnostics, January 2026. https://aoadx.com/wp-content/uploads/2026/01/Follow-the-Exits-Womens-Health-Jan-2026.pdf.

Arizton Advisory & Intelligence. *Global FemTech Market – Focused Insights 2024-2029.* Chicago: Arizton, 2024. https://www.arizton.com/market-reports/femtech-market-size

Australian Institute of Health and Welfare. *Australia's Mothers and Babies 2021.* Canberra: AIHW, 2023. https://www.aihw.gov.au/reports/mothers-babies/australias-mothers-babies.

Balas, E. A., and S. A. Boren. "Managing Clinical Knowledge for Health

Care Improvement." In *Yearbook of Medical Informatics 2000*: Patient-Centered Systems, edited by Jan H. van Bemmel and Alexa T. McCray, 65–70. Stuttgart: Schattauer, 2000. https://pubmed.ncbi.nlm.nih.gov/27699347/.

Banco, Darcy, Jerway Chang, Nina Talmor, Priya Wadhera, Amrita Mukhopadhyay, Xinlin Lu, Siyuan Dong, et al. "Sex and Race Differences in the Evaluation and Treatment of Young Adults Presenting to the Emergency Department With Chest Pain." *Journal of the American Heart Association* 11, no. 10 (May 17, 2022): e024199. https://doi.org/10.1161/JAHA.121.024199.

Bjorkman Nyqvist, Martina, Andrea Guariso, Jakob Svensson, and David Yanagizawa-Drott. "Reducing Child Mortality in the Last Mile: Experimental Evidence from Uganda." *American Economic Journal: Applied Economics* 11, no. 3 (2019): 155–192. https://www.aeaweb.org/articles?id=10.1257/app.20170201

Bloom, David E., and David Canning. "The Health and Wealth of Nations." *Science* 287, no. 5456 (2000): 1207–1209. https://doi.org/10.1126/science.287.5456.1207.

Bloom, David E., David Canning, and Jaypee Sevilla. "The Effect of Health on Economic Growth: A Production Function Approach." *World Development* 32, no. 1 (2004): 1–13. https://doi.org/10.1016/j.worlddev.2003.07.002.

Bloom, David E., Elizabeth T. Cafiero, Eva Jané-Llopis, Shafika Abrahams-Gessel, Lakshmi Reddy Bloom, Sana Fathima, Andrea B. Feigl, et al. *The Global Economic Burden of Non-Communicable Diseases.* Geneva: World Economic Forum and Harvard School of Public Health, 2011. https://www3.weforum.org/docs/WEF_Harvard_HE_GlobalEconomicBurdenNonCommunicableDiseases_2011.pdf.

Boston Consulting Group. "How Diverse Leadership Teams Boost Innovation." Boston: Boston Consulting Group, 2018. https://www.bcg.com/publications/2018/how-diverse-leadership-teams-boost-innovation.

BRAC. *Annual Report 2024-2025*. Dhaka: BRAC, 2026. https://dgikh81ssvyrj.cloudfront.net/media/documents/BRAC_Annual_Report_2024-25_1.pdf.

Breast Cancer Early Detection Coalition. https://www.bcearlydetectioncoalition.org/.

Buolamwini, Joy, and Timnit Gebru. "Gender Shades: Intersectional Accuracy Disparities in Commercial Gender Classification." *Proceedings of Machine Learning Research* 81 (2018): 1–15. http://proceedings.mlr.press/v81/buolamwini18a.html.

Butterfly Network. https://www.butterflynetwork.com/.

Canadian Institutes of Health Research. https://cihr-irsc.gc.ca/e/50837.html.

CarePay (M-TIBA). https://www.carepay.com/mtiba.

Case, Anne, Christina Paxson, and Joseph Ableidinger. "Orphans in Africa:

Parental Death, Poverty, and School Enrollment." *Demography* 41, no. 3 (2004): 483–508. http://www.jstor.org/stable/1515189.

Centers for Disease Control and Prevention. "Maternal Mortality Review Committees." Atlanta: Centers for Disease Control and Prevention, updated 2024. https://www.cdc.gov/maternal-mortality/php/mmrc/index.html.

Centers for Disease Control and Prevention. "Maternal Mortality Rates in the United States, 2024." Atlanta: Centers for Disease Control and Prevention, updated 2026. https://www.cdc.gov/nchs/data/hestat/hestat113.htm.

Chen, Brian X. "Apple's Health App Doesn't Track Menstrual Cycles." *The New York Times*, September 18, 2014. https://www.nytimes.com/2014/09/19/technology/personaltech/apple-health-app-doesnt-track-menstrual-cycles.html.

Christensen, Clayton M., Richard Alton, Curtis Rising, and Andrew Waldeck. "The Big Idea: The New M&A Playbook." *Harvard Business Review* 89, no. 3 (2011): 48–57. https://hbr.org/2011/03/the-big-idea-the-new-ma-playbook.

Clark, Helen, Awa Marie Coll-Seck, Anshu Banerjee, Stefan Peterson, Sarah L. Dalglish, Shanthi Ameratunga, Dina Balabanova, et al. "A Future for the World's Children? A WHO–UNICEF–Lancet Commission." *The Lancet* 395, no. 10224 (February 22, 2020): 605–658. https://doi.org/10.1016/S0140-6736(19)32540-1.

Cure Cervical Cancer. https://curecervicalcancer.org/.

CVS Health – "Women's Health Care." https://www.cvshealth.com/services/health-care-and-wellness/other-health-care-services/womens-health-care.html.

Deloitte. *Women @ Work 2023*: A Global Outlook. Deloitte Global, 2023. https://www.deloitte.com/global/en/issues/work/women-at-work-global-outlook.html.

DenseBreast-info, Inc.. https://densebreast-info.org/.

Diab, Adeline, and Cindy Lam. *Women Capital 2025: Gender Diversity Delivers Returns, Defies Glass Ceiling*. Bloomberg Intelligence, December 9, 2024. https://assets.bbhub.io/professional/sites/41/Women-Capital-2025.pdf.

Donner, Jonathan, and Tapan Parikh. "M-Banking and M-Payments Services in the Developing World: Complements or Substitutes for Trust and Social Capital?" *Information Technologies and International Development* 4, no. 1 (2007): 1–9. https://kiwanja.net/database/document/report_m-banking.pdf.

Ellis, Katherine, Deborah Munro, and Jennifer Clarke. "Endometriosis Is Undervalued: A Call to Action." *Frontiers in Global Women's Health* 3 (May 10, 2022): 902371. https://doi.org/10.3389/fgwh.2022.902371.

Epstein, Sherise, Emily H. Sparer, Bao N. Tran, Quing Z. Ruan, Jack

T. Dennerlein, Dhruv Singhal, and Bernard T. Lee. “Prevalence of Work-Related Musculoskeletal Disorders Among Surgeons and Interventionalists: A Systematic Review and Meta-analysis.” *JAMA Surgery* 153, no. 2 (2018): e174947. https://doi.org/10.1001/jamasurg.2017.4947.

European Commission. “Gender Equality in Research and Innovation.” European Commission Research and Innovation Strategy. Accessed 2026. https://research-and-innovation.ec.europa.eu/strategy/strategy-research-and-innovation/democracy-and-rights/gender-equality-research-and-innovation_en.

Fairweather, DeLisa, and Noel R. Rose. “Women and Autoimmune Diseases.” *Emerging Infectious Diseases* 10, no. 11 (2004): 2005–2011. https://doi.org/10.3201/eid1011.040367.

Faubion, Stephanie S., Felicity Enders, Mary S. Hedges, Rajeev Chaudhry, Juliana M. Kling, Chrisandra L. Shufelt, Mariam Saadedine, et al. “The Economic Burden of Menopause: Healthcare Utilization and Productivity Losses in the United States.” Mayo Clinic Proceedings 98, no. 6 (2023): 1014–1023. https://doi.org/10.1016/j.mayocp.2023.02.025.

Fawcett Society. *Menopause and the Workplace.* London: Fawcett Society, 2022. https://www.fawcettsociety.org.uk/menopause-and-the-workplace.

Ferry, Amy V., Atul Anand, Fiona E. Strachan, Leanne Mooney, Stacey D. Stewart, Lucy Marshall, Andrew R. Chapman, et al. “Presenting Symptoms in Men and Women Diagnosed With Myocardial Infarction Using Sex-Specific Criteria.” *Journal of the American Heart Association,* 2019. https://doi.org/10.1161/jaha.119.012307.

Gavi, the Vaccine Alliance. “Human Papillomavirus Vaccine Support.” Geneva: Gavi, updated 2023. https://www.gavi.org/types-support/vaccine-support/human-papillomavirus.

GE Healthcare. https://www.gehealthcare.com/en-us.

Ginsburg, Ruth Bader, and Amanda L. Tyler. *Justice, Justice Thou Shalt Pursue: A Life's Work Fighting for a More Perfect Union.* Berkeley: University of California Press, 2021.

Global Burden of Disease Collaborative Network. “GBD Results Tool – Migraine Disability Data.” Seattle: Institute for Health Metrics and Evaluation, 2019. http://ghdx.healthdata.org/gbd-results-tool.

Global Financing Facility for Women, Children and Adolescents. *Guidance Note: Investment Cases.* Washington, DC: Global Financing Facility, February 2016. https://www.globalfinancingfacility.org/sites/default/files/Investment%20Case%20Guidance%20Note_EN.pdf.

Global Innovation Fund. https://www.globalinnovation.fund/.

Government of the United Kingdom. *Women's Health Strategy for England.* London: Department of Health and Social Care, 2022. https://www.gov.uk/government/publications/womens-health-strategy-for-england.

Graham, L, B.J. G. Illingworth, M. Showell, M. Vercoe, E.J. Crosbie, L.J. Gingel, C.M. Farquhar, et al. "Research Priority Setting in Women's Health: A Systematic Review." *BJOG: An International Journal of Obstetrics and Gynaecology* 127, no. 6 (May 2020): 694–700. https://doi.org/10.1111/1471-0528.16150.

GSMA Connected Women. *The Mobile Gender Gap Report 2023*. London: GSMA, 2023. https://www.gsma.com/r/gender-gap/.

Guttmacher Institute. *Adding It Up: Investing in Sexual and Reproductive Health 2019*. New York: Guttmacher Institute, 2020. https://www.guttmacher.org/report/adding-it-up-investing-in-sexual-reproductive-health-2019.

Hall, Michaela T., Kate T. Simms, Jie-Bin Lew, Megan A. Smith, Julia M.L. Brotherton, Marion Saville, Ian H. Frazer, et al. "The Projected Timeframe Until Cervical Cancer Elimination in Australia: A Modelling Study." *The Lancet Public Health* 4, no. 1 (2019): e19–e27. https://doi.org/10.1016/S2468-2667(18)30183-X.

Hamoda, Haitham, Nick Panay, Hugo Pedder, Roopen Arya, and Mike Savvasl. "The British Menopause Society & Women's Health Concern Recommendations on the Management of Menopausal Symptoms." *Post Reproductive Health*, updated guidance. https://doi.org/10.1177/2053369120957514.

Hanton, Thomas, Kelsey Lennox, Fran Carroll, John Allotey, Wessel Ganzevoort, Sanne Gordijn, and Asma Khalil. Women's Health Research Priorities (WHRP): A UK-Based Consensus to Identify the Priorities for Research That Matter Most to Women. London: Royal College of Obstetricians & Gynaecologists, December 2025. https://www.rcog.org.uk/media/ekrlccyg/womens-health-research-priorities_dec-2025.pdf.

Healy, Bernadine. "The Yentl Syndrome." *New England Journal of Medicine* 325, no. 4 (1991): 274–276. https://doi.org/10.1056/nejm199107253250408.

Heise, Lori, Margaret E. Greene, Neisha Opper, Maria Stavropoulou, Caroline Harper, Marcos Nascimento, and Debrework Zewdie. "Gender Inequality and Restrictive Gender Norms: Framing the Challenges to Health." *The Lancet* 393, no. 10189 (2019): 2440–2454. https://www.thelancet.com/journals/lancet/article/PIIS0140-6736(19)30652-X/fulltext.

HERhealthEQ. https://www.herhealtheq.org.

Hippensteele, Alana. "Investment Trends in Women's Health Are Driving Growth in Health Care Innovation." Presentation at Asembia's AXS24 Summit, Las Vegas. Pharmacy Times, 2024. https://www.pharmacytimes.com/view/investment-trends-in-women-s-health-are-driving-growth-in-health-care-innovation.

Hologic. https://www.hologic.com/.

Impact Global Health. Impact Global Health Data. London: Impact Global Health. https://www.impactglobalhealth.org/data.

Institute for Health Metrics and Evaluation. Health Financing. Seattle: Institute for Health Metrics and Evaluation. https://www.healthdata.org/research-analysis/health-financing.

Insulet Corporation. https://www.insulet.com/.

International Agency for Research on Cancer. "Cancer Today: Breast Cancer Fact Sheet." Lyon: International Agency for Research on Cancer, 2020. https://gco.iarc.who.int/media/globocan/factsheets/cancers/20-breast-fact-sheet.pdf.

International Agency for Research on Cancer. Global Cancer Observatory (GLOBOCAN 2020). Lyon: International Agency for Research on Cancer, 2020. https://gco.iarc.who.int/today/en/fact-sheets-cancers.

International Labour Organization. *Care Work and Care Jobs for the Future of Decent Work*. Geneva: International Labour Organization, 2018. https://www.ilo.org/global/publications/books/WCMS_633135/lang--en/index.htm.

International Monetary Fund. *World Economic Outlook: Recovery During a Pandemic: Health Concerns, Supply Disruptions, and Price Pressures*. Washington, DC: International Monetary Fund, 2021. https://www.imf.org/en/Publications/WEO/Issues/2021/10/12/world-economic-outlook-october-2021.

International Orthopaedic Diversity Alliance. "Diversity in Orthopaedics and Traumatology: A Global Perspective." EFORT Open Reviews 5, no. 10 (October 26, 2020): 743–752. https://doi.org/10.1302/2058-5241.5.200022.

International Osteoporosis Foundation. "Fragility Fractures." Nyon, Switzerland: International Osteoporosis Foundation, updated 2023. https://www.osteoporosis.foundation/health-professionals/fragility-fractures.

International Osteoporosis Foundation. "Osteoporosis Facts and Statistics." Nyon, Switzerland: International Osteoporosis Foundation, updated 2023. https://www.osteoporosis.foundation/facts-statistics.

Jacaranda Health. https://jacarandahealth.org/.

Jack, William, and Tavneet Suri. "Mobile Money: The Economics of M-Pesa." *NBER Working Paper* No. 16721. Cambridge, MA: National Bureau of Economic Research, 2011. https://doi.org/10.3386/w16721.

Jhpiego. https://jhpiego.org/.

Jin, Xurui, Chanchal Chandramouli, Brooke Allocco, Enying Gong, Carolyn S.P. Lam, and Lijing L. Yan. "Women's Participation in Cardiovascular Clinical Trials From 2010 to 2017." *Circulation* 141, no. 7 (2020): 540–548. https://doi.org/10.1161/CIRCULATIONAHA.119.043594.

Johnson, Ari D., Oumar Thiero, Caroline Whidden, Belco Poudiougou, Djoumé, Fousséni Traore, Salif Samaké, et al. "Proactive Community Case Management and Child Survival in Periurban Mali." *BMJ Global Health* 3, no. 2 (2018): e000634. https://gh.bmj.com/content/3/2/e000634.

Kaiser Family Foundation. "Medicaid Postpartum Coverage Extension Tracker." Kaiser Family Foundation, updated 2024. https://www.kff.org/medicaid/issue-brief/medicaid-postpartum-coverage-extension-tracker/.

Kemble, Emma, Lucy Pérez, Valentina Sartori, Gila Tolub, and Alice Zheng. "Unlocking Opportunities in Women's Healthcare." McKinsey & Company, February 14, 2022. https://www.mckinsey.com/industries/healthcare/our-insights/unlocking-opportunities-in-womens-healthcare.

Kimi. https://kimi.bf/.

KPMG. *The M&A Dance: Orchestrating Synergies and Value Creation in Public Company Acquisitions.* KPMG International, 2025. https://assets.kpmg.com/content/dam/kpmgsites/xx/pdf/2025/08/ma-dance.pdf.coredownload.inline.pdf.

The Lancet. "Time to Listen to Women about Their Pain." Editorial. *The Lancet Rheumatology* 6, no. 6 (June 2024): e329. https://doi.org/10.1016/S2665-9913(24)00126-7.

Langer, Ana, Afaf Meleis, Felicia M. Knaul, Rifat Atun, Meltem Aran, Héctor Arreola-Ornelas, Zulfiqar A. Bhutta, et al. "Women and Health: The Key for Sustainable Development." *The Lancet* 386, no. 9999 (September 19, 2015): 1165–1210. https://doi.org/10.1016/S0140-6736(15)60497-4.

Lau, K. H. Vincent, Pria Anand, Alex Ramirez, and Sheila Phicil. "Disparities in Telehealth Use During the COVID-19 Pandemic." *Journal of Immigrant and Minority Health* 24, no. 6 (December 2022): 1590–1593. https://doi.org/10.1007/s10903-022-01381-1.

Larrazabal, Agostina J., Nicolás Nieto, Victoria Peterson, Diego H. Milone, and Enzo Ferrante. "Gender Imbalance in Medical Imaging Datasets Produces Biased Classifiers for Computer-Aided Diagnosis." *Proceedings of the National Academy of Sciences* 117, no. 23 (2020): 12592–12594. https://www.pnas.org/doi/10.1073/pnas.1919012117.

Lawson, Max, Anam Parvez Butt, Rowan Harvey, Diana Sarosi, Clare Coffey, Kim Piaget, and Julie Thekkudan. "Time to Care: Unpaid and Underpaid Care Work and the Global Inequality Crisis." Oxford: Oxfam, 2020. https://www.oxfam.org/en/research/time-care.

The Lens Intelligence. "Insight Engine Survey." https://www.thelensintelligence.com/insightsenginesurvey.

LifeBank. https://lifebankcares.com/.

Living Goods. https://livinggoods.org/.

M-TIBA. https://mtiba.com/.

Macrotrends. "Insulet (PODD) Revenue History 2012-2026." https://www.macrotrends.net/stocks/charts/PODD/insulet/revenue.

Mandela, Nelson. *Long Walk to Freedom: The Autobiography of Nelson Mandela.* Boston: Little, Brown and Company, 1994.

The Max Foundation. https://themaxfoundation.org/.

The Max Foundation. *Leading the Way: Advancing Our Impact in 2024.* 2024 Annual Report. Seattle: The Max Foundation, 2025. https://themaxfoundation.org/advancing-our-impact-in-2024/.

McKinsey & Company. "Diversity Wins: How Inclusion Matters." McKinsey & Company, 2020. https://www.mckinsey.com/featured-insights/diversity-and-inclusion/diversity-wins-how-inclusion-matters.

McKinsey Global Institute. "The Power of Parity: How Advancing Women's Equality Can Add $12 Trillion to Global Growth." McKinsey & Company, 2015. https://www.mckinsey.com/featured-insights/employment-and-growth/how-advancing-womens-equality-can-add-12-trillion-to-global-growth.

McKinsey Health Institute. "Closing the Women's Health Gap: A $1 Trillion Opportunity to Improve Lives and Economies." McKinsey & Company, 2024. https://www.mckinsey.com/mhi/our-insights/closing-the-womens-health-gap-a-1-trillion-dollar-opportunity-to-improve-lives-and-economies.

Miller, Leah R., Cheryl Marks, Jill B. Becker, Patricia D. Hurn, Wei-Jung Chen, Teresa Woodruff, Margaret M. McCarthy, et al. "Considering Sex as a Biological Variable in Preclinical Research." FASEB Journal 31, no. 1 (2017): 29–34. https://doi.org/10.1096/fj.201600781R.

Ministry of Health, Rwanda. *The National Digital Health Strategic Plan 2018–2023.* Kigali: Government of Rwanda, 2018. https://extranet.who.int/countryplanningcycles/sites/default/files/public_file_rep/RWA_Rwanda_Digital-Health-Strategy_2018-2023.Pdf.

Mnookin, Seth. *Out of the shadows: Making Mental Health a Global Development Priority (English).* Washington, D.C.: World Bank Group. 2016. http://documents.worldbank.org/curated/en/270131468187759113

Morgan, Rosemary, Anna Kalbarczyk, Diwakar Mohan, Choolwe Jacobs, Manasee Mishra, Prakash Tyagi, Cindy Cox-Roman, et al. "Counting Older Women: Measuring the Health and Wellbeing of Older Women in LMICs." *Cell Reports Medicine* 5, no. 6 (June 18, 2024): 101607. https://doi.org/10.1016/j.xcrm.2024.101607.

mPharma. https://mpharma.com/.

MSCI. *Women on Boards: Progress Report 2017*. MSCI ESG Research, 2017. https://www.msci.com/documents/10199/239004/MSCI_Women+on+Boards+Progress+Report+2017.pdf.

Murthy, Vivek H., Harlan M. Krumholz, and Cary P. Gross. "Participation in Cancer Clinical Trials: Race-, Sex-, and Age-Based Disparities." *JAMA* 291, no. 22 (2004): 2720–2726. https://doi.org/10.1001/jama.291.22.2720.

Muso Health. https://www.musohealth.org/.

Muso. "Proactive Care Model: Reports and Evidence Hub." https://www.musohealth.org/research.

Nantume, Assumpta, Sona Shah, Teresa Cauvel, Matthew Tomback, Ryan Kilpatrick, Bushra Afzal, and Noah Kiwanuka. "Developing Medical Technologies for Low-Resource Settings: Lessons From a Wireless Wearable Vital Signs Monitor-neoGuard." *Frontiers in Digital Health* 3 (October 15, 2021): 730951. https://doi.org/10.3389/fdgth.2021.730951.

Nantume, Assumpta, Bertha Akinyi Oketch, Dickson Otiangala, Sona Shah, Teresa Cauvel, Boniface Nyumbile, and Bernard Olayo. "Feasibility, Performance and Acceptability of an Innovative Vital Signs Monitor for Sick Newborns in Western Kenya: A Mixed-Methods Study." *Digital Health* 9 (June 26, 2023): 20552076231182799. https://doi.org/10.1177/20552076231182799.

Narayana Health. https://www.narayanahealth.org/.

National Academies of Sciences, Engineering, and Medicine. *A New Vision for Women's Health Research: Transformative Change at the National Institutes of Health.* Edited by Sheila P. Burke, Alina Salganicoff, and Amy Geller. Washington, DC: National Academies Press, 2025. https://doi.org/10.17226/28586.

National Institute for Health and Care Excellence. "Menopause: Identification and Management." NICE Guideline NG23. London: NICE. https://www.nice.org.uk/guidance/ng23.

National Institute of Mental Health. "Women and Mental Health." Bethesda, MD: National Institute of Mental Health. https://www.nimh.nih.gov/health/topics/women-and-mental-health.

National Institutes of Health, Office of Research on Women's Health. "Federal Focus on Women's Health Research." Bethesda, MD: NIH. https://orwh.od.nih.gov/archive/federal-focus-on-womens-health-research.

National Institutes of Health, Office of Research on Women's Health. *NIH-Wide Strategic Plan for Women's Health Research.* Bethesda, MD: NIH. https://orwh.od.nih.gov/about/strategic-plan.

Neopenda. https://www.neopenda.com/.

Nielsen, Mathias Wullum, Sharla Algeria, Love Börjeson, Henry Etzkowitz, Holly J. Falk-Krzesinski, Aparna Joshi, Erin Leahey, et al. "Opinion: Gender Diversity Leads to Better Science." *Proceedings of the National Academy of Sciences* 114, no. 8 (2017): 1740–1742. https://www.pnas.org/doi/10.1073/pnas.1700616114.

Nnoaham, Kelechi E., Lone Hummelshoj, Premila Webster, Thomas d'Hooghe, Fiorenzo de Cicco Nardone, Carlo de Cicco Nardone, Crispin Jenkinson, et al. "Impact of Endometriosis on Quality of Life and Work Productivity: A Multicenter Study Across Ten Countries." *Fertility and Sterility* 96, no. 2 (2011): 366-373.e8. https://doi.org/10.1016/j.fertnstert.2011.05.090.

Noland, Marcus, Tyler Moran, and Barbara Kotschwar. "Is Gender Diversity Profitable? Evidence From a Global Survey." Peterson Institute for International Economics Working Paper 16-3, 2016. https://www.piie.

com/publications/working-papers/gender-diversity-profitable-evidence-global-survey.

Office of Research on Women's Health. "History of Women's Participation in Clinical Research." NIH Inclusion Outreach Toolkit. National Institutes of Health. Last updated April 24, 2024. https://orwh.od.nih.gov/toolkit/recruitment/history.

Organisation for Economic Co-operation and Development. "A Historic Decline in Foreign Aid: Preliminary 2025 ODA Data." OECD Data Insights, April 2026. https://www.oecd.org/en/data/insights/data-explainers/2026/04/a-historic-decline-in-foreign-aid-preliminary-2025-oda-data.html.

Organon. https://www.organon.com/.

Perez, Caroline Criado. *Invisible Women: Data Bias in a World Designed for Men.* New York: Abrams Press, 2019.

PharmAccess Foundation. https://www.pharmaccess.org/.

Pivotal Ventures. https://www.pivotal.com/.

Portfolia. https://www.portfolia.co/.

Post, Corinne, and Kris Byron. "Women on Boards and Firm Financial Performance: A Meta-Analysis." *Academy of Management Journal* 58, no. 5 (2015): 1546–1571. https://doi.org/10.5465/amj.2013.0319.

Post, Corinne, Noushi Rahman, and Emily Rubow. "Green Governance: Boards of Directors' Composition and Environmental Corporate Social Responsibility." *Business & Society* 50, no. 1 (2011): 189–223. https://journals.sagepub.com/doi/10.1177/0007650310394642.

Psacharopoulos, George, and Harry Anthony Patrinos. "Returns to Investment in Education: A Decennial Review of the Global Literature." *Education Economics* 26, no. 5 (2018): 445–458. https://doi.org/10.1080/09645292.2018.1484426.

Regensteiner, Judith G., Melissa McNeil, Stephanie S. Faubion, C. Noel Bairey-Merz, Martha Gulati, Hadine Joffe, Rita F. Redberg, et al. "Barriers and Solutions in Women's Health Research and Clinical Care: A Call to Action." *The Lancet Regional Health – Americas* 44 (April 2025): 101037. https://doi.org/10.1016/j.lana.2025.101037.

Rockefeller Foundation. "Africa in the Driver's Seat." Bellagio Breakthroughs. The Rockefeller Foundation, 2026. https://www.rockefellerfoundation.org/bellagio-breakthroughs/africa-in-the-drivers-seat/.

Safaricom. https://www.safaricom.co.ke/.

Shekar, Meera, Jakub Kakietek, Julia Dayton Eberwein, and Dylan Walters. *An Investment Framework for Nutrition: Reaching the Global Targets for Stunting, Anemia, Breastfeeding, and Wasting.* Directions in Development—Human Development. Washington, DC: World Bank, 2017. http://hdl.handle.net/10986/26069.

Sjoding, Michael W., Robert P. Dickson, Theodore J. Iwashyna, Steven E. Gay, and Thomas S. Valley. "Racial Bias in Pulse Oximetry Measurement." *New England Journal of Medicine* 383, no. 25 (2020): 2477–2478. https://doi.org/10.1056/NEJMc2029240.

Stenberg, Karin, Henrik Axelson, Peter Sheehan, Ian Anderson, A. Metin Gülmezoglu, Marleen Temmerman, Elizabeth Mason, et al. "Advancing Social and Economic Development by Investing in Women's and Children's Health: A New Global Investment Framework." *The Lancet* 383, no. 9925 (2014): 1333-1354. https://doi.org/10.1016/S0140-6736(13)62231-X.

Sung, Hyuna, Jacques Ferlay, Rebecca L. Siegel, Mathieu Laversanne, Isabelle Soerjomataram, Ahmedin Jemal, and Freddie Bray. "Global Cancer Statistics 2020: GLOBOCAN Estimates of Incidence and Mortality Worldwide for 36 Cancers in 185 Countries." *CA: A Cancer Journal for Clinicians* 71, no. 3 (2021): 209–249. https://doi.org/10.3322/caac.21660.

Suri, Tavneet, and William Jack. "The Long-Run Poverty and Gender Impacts of Mobile Money." *Science* 354, no. 6317 (2016): 1288–1292. https://www.science.org/doi/10.1126/science.aah5309.

U.S. General Accounting Office. "National Institutes of Health: Problems in Implementing Policy on Women in Study Populations." GAO/T-HRD-90-50. Testimony of Mark V. Nadel before the Subcommittee on Housing and Consumer Interest, Select Committee on Aging, House of Representatives. Washington, DC: U.S. General Accounting Office, July 24, 1990. https://www.gao.gov/products/t-hrd-90-50.

U.S. House of Representatives, "United States Representative Rosa L. DeLauro." https://delauro.house.gov.

Ultrasound AI. https://ultrasound.ai/.

United Nations Children's Fund. "Harnessing the Power of Data for Girls: Taking Stock and Looking Ahead to 2030." New York: UNICEF, 2016. https://data.unicef.org/resources/harnessing-the-power-of-data-for-girls/.

United Nations Population Fund. "Child Marriage." New York: UNFPA, 2020. https://www.unfpa.org/child-marriage.

United Nations Population Fund. *Seeing the Unseen: The Case for Action in the Neglected Crisis of Unintended Pregnancy.* New York: UNFPA, 2022. https://www.unfpa.org/swp2022.

United Nations Population Fund. "World Population Dashboard: Unmet Need for Family Planning." New York: UNFPA. https://www.unfpa.org/data/world-population-dashboard#unmet-need-for-family-planning.

United Nations, Department of Economic and Social Affairs, Population Division. *World Population Ageing 2020: Highlights.* New York: United Nations, 2020. https://www.un.org/development/desa/pd/content/world-population-ageing-2020-highlights.

United Nations, Department of Economic and Social Affairs, Population Division. "World Population Prospects." New York: United Nations, 2022. https://population.un.org/wpp.

Vogel, Birgit, Monica Acevedo, Yolande Appelman, C. Noel Bairey Merz, Alaide Chieffo, Gemma A Figtree, Mayra Guerrero, et al. "The Lancet Women and Cardiovascular Disease Commission: Reducing the Global Burden by 2030." *The Lancet* 397, no. 10292 (2021): 2385–2438. https://www.thelancet.com/article/S0140-6736(21)00684-X/fulltext.

Vos, Theo, Stephen S. Lim, Cristiana Abbafati, Kaja M. Abbas, Mohammad Abbasi, Mitra Abbasifard, Mohsen Abbasi-Kangevari, et al. "Global Burden of 369 Diseases and Injuries in 204 Countries and Territories, 1990–2019: A Systematic Analysis for the Global Burden of Disease Study 2019." *The Lancet* 396, no. 10258 (2020): 1204–1222. https://doi.org/10.1016/S0140-6736(20)30925-9.

Weckman, Andrea M., and Patricia Farrugia. "Inequities in Canadian maternal-child healthcare are perpetuating the intergenerational effects of colonization for indigenous women and children." *Frontiers in Global Women's Health* 6 (2025): 1513145. https://doi.org/10.3389/fgwh.2025.1513145.

Wenham, Clare, Julia Smith, and Rosemary Morgan. "COVID-19: The Gendered Impacts of the Outbreak." *The Lancet* 395, no. 10227 (2020): 846–848. https://doi.org/10.1016/S0140-6736(20)30526-2.

Women in Global Health. https://womeningh.org/.

Women's Health Advocates. https://womenshealthadvocates.org/.

Women's Health Innovation Coalition. https://womenshealthinnovation.org/.

Women's Health Network. https://thewomenshealthnetwork.org/.

Women's Health PAC. https://womenshealthpac.us/.

World Bank. "Missed Opportunities: The High Cost of Not Educating Girls." Washington, DC: World Bank, 2018. https://www.worldbank.org/en/topic/education/publication/missed-opportunities-the-high-cost-of-not-educating-girls.

World Bank. *Women, Business and the Law 2023.* Washington, DC: World Bank, 2023. https://doi.org/10.1596/978-1-4648-1944-5.

World Economic Forum. *Global Gender Gap Report 2023.* Geneva: World Economic Forum, 2023. https://www.weforum.org/reports/global-gender-gap-report-2023.

World Health Organization and World Bank. *Tracking Universal Health Coverage: 2023 Global Monitoring Report.* Geneva: World Health Organization, 2023. https://www.who.int/publications/i/item/9789240080379.

World Health Organization, UNICEF, UNFPA, World Bank Group, and UN DESA. *Trends in Maternal Mortality 2000–2020.* Geneva: World

Health Organization, 2023. https://www.who.int/publications/i/item/9789240068759.

World Health Organization. "Cardiovascular Diseases (CVDs)." Geneva: World Health Organization, updated 2023. https://www.who.int/news-room/fact-sheets/detail/cardiovascular-diseases-(cvds).

World Health Organization. "Cervical Cancer." Geneva: World Health Organization, updated 2024. https://www.who.int/news-room/fact-sheets/detail/cervical-cancer.

World Health Organization. *Comprehensive Cervical Cancer Control: A Guide to Essential Practice.* 2nd ed. Geneva: World Health Organization, 2014. https://www.who.int/publications/i/item/9789241548953.

World Health Organization. *Delivered by Women, Led by Men: A Gender and Equity Analysis of the Global Health and Social Workforce.* Geneva: World Health Organization, 2019. https://www.who.int/publications/i/item/9789241515467.

World Health Organization. *Depression and Other Common Mental Disorders: Global Health Estimates.* Geneva: World Health Organization, 2017. https://www.who.int/publications/i/item/depression-global-health-estimates.

World Health Organization. "Depressive disorder (depression)." Fact sheet. 29 August 2025. https://www.who.int/news-room/fact-sheets/detail/depression.

World Health Organization. "Endometriosis." Geneva: World Health Organization. https://www.who.int/news-room/fact-sheets/detail/endometriosis.

World Health Organization. *Global Spending on Health: Rising to the Pandemic's Challenges.* Geneva: World Health Organization, 2022. https://www.who.int/publications/i/item/9789240064911.

World Health Organization. *Global Strategy to Accelerate the Elimination of Cervical Cancer as a Public Health Problem.* Geneva: World Health Organization, 2020. https://www.who.int/publications/i/item/9789240014107.

World Health Organization. "Menopause." Fact Sheet. Geneva: World Health Organization, updated 2023. https://www.who.int/news-room/fact-sheets/detail/menopause.

World Health Organization. *Noncommunicable Diseases Progress Monitor 2022.* Geneva: World Health Organization, 2022. https://www.who.int/publications/i/item/9789240047761.

World Health Organization. "Noncommunicable Diseases." Geneva: World Health Organization, updated 2023. https://www.who.int/news-room/fact-sheets/detail/noncommunicable-diseases.

World Health Organization. *WHO Consolidated Guideline on Self-Care Interventions for Health and Well-Being.* Geneva: World Health

Organization, 2022 update. https://www.who.int/publications/i/item/9789240052192.

World Health Organization. *World Health Statistics 2023: Monitoring Health for the SDGs.* Geneva: World Health Organization, 2023. https://www.who.int/publications/i/item/9789240074323.

Wu, Pensée, Randula Haththotuwa, Chun Shing Kwok, Aswin Babu, Rafail A. Kotronias, Claire Rushton, Azfar Zaman, et al. "Preeclampsia and Future Cardiovascular Health: A Systematic Review and Meta-Analysis." *Circulation: Population Health and Outcomes* 10, no. 2 (2017): e003497. https://doi.org/10.1161/CIRCOUTCOMES.116.003497.

Younes, Samer. "The relationship between gender and pharmacology." *Current Research in Pharmacology and Drug Discovery* 7 (2024): 100192. https://doi.org/10.1016/j.crphar.2024.100192.

Zipline. https://www.zipline.com/.

ABOUT THE AUTHOR

Marissa Fayer is a four-time venture-backed medtech CEO and a twenty-five-year operator in the women's health space who has raised capital, managed P&Ls, navigated FDA approvals, and built distribution channels across five continents. She's been named to the Top 100 Women in Medtech, a First in FemTech honoree, and a MedTech Voice to Watch.

She spent the first half of her career in executive roles at Hologic, Olympus, and Maquet Getinge, living and working across the US, Canada, Mexico, and Costa Rica. One night in Costa Rica, a friend told her that women on the coast were dying of breast cancer because the region's only mammography unit had been broken for years. She found a repurposed machine in a US warehouse and worked with the government, the US Embassy, and a local hospital to get it installed. Several years later, the mortality rate in that region dropped tenfold. That's how HERhealthEQ was born. The nonprofit has since reached more than 135,000 women across twelve countries.

She is currently CEO of DeepLook Medical, an FDA-cleared AI diagnostics company focused on breast cancer detection in women with dense breast tissue, a condition she has herself. She's a World Economic Forum Technology Fellow 2026-2028, an investment committee member at GG Ventures, and a founding member of the Milken Institute's Women's Health Committee.

Undervalued to Unavoidable is her first book. She wrote it because the capital, the science, and the market are all there. The infrastructure isn't. Learn more at marissafayer.com.

www.ingramcontent.com/pod-product-compliance
Ingram Content Group UK Ltd.
Pitfield, Milton Keynes, MK11 3LW, UK
UKHW021838270726
14058UKWH00002B/222